this i know

notes on unraveling the heart

SUSANNAH CONWAY

Guilford, Connecticut
An imprint of Globe Pequot Press

To buy books in quantity for corporate use
or incentives, call **(800) 962-0973**
or e-mail **premiums@GlobePequot.com**.

 skirt!® is an attitude . . . spirited, independent, outspoken, serious, playful and irreverent, sometimes controversial, always passionate.

Text design and layout: Sheryl P. Kober
Project editor: Kristen Mellitt

Library of Congress Cataloging-in-Publication Data is available on file.

ISBN 978-0-7627-7008-3

Printed in China

10 9 8 7 6 5 4 3 2

To my mother, Diane; my sister, Abby; and my nephew, Noah.

You three are my heart.

contents

Introduction ix

1. An ending, a beginning 1

2. The tides 27

3. Redrafting the blueprint 51

4. Writing with my eyes 71

5. I have a body 93

6. Look me in the eye and tell me you don't love me 119

7. A tribe of one 145

8. The art of belonging 169

9. Unraveled 193

Epilogue 220

Book Friends 226

Love & Gratitude 231

About the Author 233

introduction

"People come and go in your life but they never leave your dreams. Once they are in your subconscious, they are immortal."

—Patricia Hampl

everything changed when the man I loved died from a sudden heart attack in the spring of 2005; in that single missing heartbeat I lost my life too. Six weeks after the funeral I left London and moved back to my hometown on the south coast of England, needing to be near my family, old friends, and the sea. The experts tell you not to make any big decisions in the first year of bereavement, but I knew that wasn't working for me. I needed to be away from the places that only served to remind me that he was gone. Sleeping in the bedroom we'd shared was not a comfort for me—it was torture. So I rented a small attic flat that was a ten-minute walk from the beach, and it was there, finally alone, finally able to let go, that I collapsed into my grief.

I made it through the first weeks in a haze of shock, an altered state that made everything excruciating: music played in shops reminded me of him; everywhere I looked I'd see his name; every call on my mobile phone was another one not from him. It was more than I could bear. As the weeks passed I retreated into myself, the outside world too abrasive on my raw skin.

There were three wise moves I made in the first eighteen months that helped me heal more than anything else. The first was to find a sympathetic doctor and ask for help. As the shock and sensitivity gave way to thick black depression, even I realized, in my numbed-out state, that there was no way I could

heal when I couldn't *feel*, so I finally reached out to a doctor, and she prescribed anti-depressants. Those small white pills were the lifeboat that helped me reach the shore and find my therapist.

I'd always been wary of therapy, considering it the pre-serve of the neurotic and desperate. Now, of course, I know better, and can honestly say without any trace of melodrama, that working with Jill saved my life. Just the simple and con-sistent practice of talking to her for one hour a week gave me my life back in ways I hadn't known I'd needed. For the first year I mainly talked—cried, vented—about my love, needing to go over and over his death, my loss, and what could have been. But as I moved into the second year I began to unravel farther back into the past. Because, you see, when something bad hap-pens that's big enough to make you question your entire life, all the other hurts that are hanging around, all the wounds you've collected during your lifetime, will come out of the shadows and ask to be healed too. It's entirely possible to squash your pain down and carry on with your life, but one day it will catch up with you. One day a little tear will appear in the blanket and then, with an almighty rip, all your crap comes tumbling out. This is a good thing in the long run.

Thirteen months after his death I made my second wise move: I started writing a blog. Although I was spending a little

Unraveling is not a bad thing. It's not coming undone or losing control. It's letting go in the best possible way, untangling the knots that hold you back, unwrapping the gifts you've hidden for too long, unearthing the potential that's always been there, finally ditching the labels and should-haves, and letting yourself be what you were always meant to be.

more time out of my house with friends and family, I still preferred to stay close to home. Discovering the blogging community was like finding the most delicious world hidden inside my computer, beckoning me to come out and play. Back in 2006 the blogosphere still felt relatively small and with a little encouragement from friends that I'd made online I jumped in and wrote my first blog post on April 12th. I'd worked as a freelance journalist back in London, so expressing myself through words came easily; soon the blog became my place to talk about my grief, writing first and foremost for myself, but also attracting readers who connected deeply with what I was sharing. The immediacy of blogging—being able to write a post, publish it, and get almost immediate feedback and support—proved to be incredibly healing, as I shared the dips and plateaus of grief, and found support in a community of writers, artists, and people just like me, sharing pieces of their day-to-day life online.

Despite the public venue, the personal nature of my blog helped me connect with women who were walking similar paths and discovering their own creative voices. I became close to six women in particular, and after months of connecting via our blogs, e-mail, and the occasional transatlantic phone call, we hatched a plan to spend a weekend together in Seattle. The trip was a significant milestone in my recovery—my first visit to the United States, the first time I was meeting these women, and my first big adventure after eighteen months of grieving. Any anxiety I felt was dwarfed by the thrill of doing something that would have been unthinkable just a year earlier.

The trip proved to be life-changing, from forging friendships for life to opening my eyes to the world around me. What had been growing over the previous months of blogging exploded when I was faced with a brand new city to explore. Walking through the rain with my new friends, I was taken out of my grief and brought squarely back into the moment. I'd borrowed a camera for the trip, and I filled the memory card by the end of the weekend—my eyes were open again.

The third wise move I made was buying a digital camera soon after I returned home. I'd studied photography for three years at art college and had a well-developed sense of aesthetics, but as I'd always shot with film cameras I had to learn a new way of working, which seemed perfectly in keeping with my new way of seeing the world. I read *The Artist's Way*, Julia Cameron's classic course in creativity, and took myself out on weekly Artist's Dates, going to new places to take photos and then posting them online when I got home. The dynamic combination of writing and photography reconnected me to my creativity in a profound way, helping me process my feelings as I healed and giving me a reason to get back out into the world. I started taking regular self-portraits as a way to see myself again—a woman on my own, no longer defined by my loss, rediscovering my artistic voice. At the beginning of 2008, I happened upon an old Polaroid camera in a street market and fell back in love with analog photography, the dreamy squares of film transcribing my eye even more accurately than my digital camera had done. My creativity positively bloomed.

Feeling ready to move on from my healing cocoon by the sea, in the autumn of 2008 I moved one hundred miles away to the historic city of Bath in southwest England. Knowing no one and without a job, I found the re-entry disorienting, but after a few months of recalibration—going out to explore my new home with my camera was essential to my sanity—I discovered exactly how healed I really was. An invitation to teach an evening class at an adult education center in the nearby city of Bristol proved to be a turning point. I'd never taught in a classroom before, but I knew I had something of value to share. Inspired by my blogging and photography over the previous three years, I pieced together notes from my many Moleskine journals and devised a class that used the camera as a tool to reconnect with the self via photo assignments and journaling exercises. It was exciting to see those first students work through the material, making their own discoveries and sharing pieces of their lives with each other.

After that first successful run, I knew I wanted to share the class with more women, and as blogging had become such an important part of my life, it made sense to offer the class online. So in January 2009 I launched the *Unravelling: Ways of Seeing My Self* e-course. That first class sold out in a week. The fourth time I offered the class it sold out in ten minutes. Word was spreading and healing was happening for women all over the world. It still amazes me that my own painstaking unraveling, undoing layer after layer to reach a place of self-acceptance, was the catalyst for something so much bigger than me. It was as if there was a purpose to my partner's death and all the pain that came after—that thought gives me enormous comfort.

When I started writing my blog I made a conscious decision not to use my partner's name in any of my posts as I felt strongly that what we'd shared was private and not to be plastered all over the Internet. I wanted to build a space that chronicled the new life I was creating while still leaving room for my memories and sadness, and the same goes for this book. This is not a story about grief, although it informs everything I've learned about life. This is a book about unraveling the layers of our lives and exploring what we find in order to better understand ourselves, our relationships, and our path. Sometimes it seems easier to go through life holding everything in, wrapped up, breath held, eyes forward, but life will always rub up against us—that's how the pearls are formed. So unraveling is not a bad thing in this context. It's not coming undone or losing control.

It's letting go in the best possible way, untangling the knots that hold you back, unwrapping the gifts you've hidden for too long, unearthing the potential that's always been there, finally ditching the labels and should-haves, and letting yourself be what you were always meant to be. That's what I did and what I continue to do to this day. Living mindfully, appreciating what I have, learning to let go of what I no longer need, and practicing kindness as often as I can—especially toward myself. Every layer I unraveled during my recovery taught me something new, and this book explores each layer in turn: how grief reshaped my life, how I found new meaning in the world around me, how I reconnected to my creativity, how I began to understand my past, and how I faced down my own reflection to try to accept the body I live in. Unraveling also helped me learn to appreciate my own company and nurture my important relationships. It is how I found my place in the world and the work I feel compelled to share.

So this is a guidebook of sorts, a collection of my thoughts and theories, illustrated with my beloved Polaroids. At the end of each chapter is a *reflection*—a small creative exercise to help you think about the ideas and stories presented in the book. I hope these pages let you see that you are not alone, that your struggles are my struggles too. I don't have the answers—I'm not sure if anyone really has the answers—but I do have a hell of a lot of questions and perhaps you do too. Some days I wake up and realize that I know absolutely nothing and that my birth certificate must be wrong because I am, in fact, still a child. But I know more than I did at twenty-one and I know more than I did last year. By the time these words are published I will know even more still; but for now, I'm going to record what I know today. As life is one long tangle of todays, this plan should work just fine. I don't worry too much about tomorrow anymore. All we have is today.

this i know for sure.

Susannah Conway

an ending, a beginning

"How could one person, not very big, leave an emptiness that was galaxy-wide?"

—Sheldon Vanauken, from *A Severe Mercy*

I am standing in my mother's kitchen, dressing a green salad with vinegar and olive oil. It's a gorgeous sunny day and we're celebrating my stepfather's sixtieth birthday with a barbeque for friends and family. I can smell the sausages cooking as the smoke winds its way through the open window. I take the salad out into the garden and leave it on the table with the bread rolls and relishes, picking up my glass of beer and heading for the chair beside my sister. It's been over eighteen months since I left London and moved back to the coast—I'm now working with a therapist and writing a blog, doing little bits of work here and there and slowly feeling like I have a life again. There are still excruciatingly raw days when I shut myself away, but today is a special day, and being with my family has buoyed my mood.

Midway through the afternoon a colleague from Mum's office arrives with his wife, and I watch as they mingle with the friends they recognize, though the smiles they wear are slightly off. I know that Roger and Christine's twenty-year-old son died in a car crash three months before I lost my love, and I often ask after them, wondering how they are coping, knowing what I now know. Mum says Roger asks after me too—I feel a connection to them, though we've never met before.

They stay for half an hour and then make their way to their car. As my mother talks to Christine, I go over to Roger to say good-bye. There is no awkwardness as I reach out and give him a hug and though we are easily twenty years apart in age, in that moment we are the same.

"It's just really awful, isn't it," I say, meaning death, meaning grief, meaning everything I know he is feeling.

"Yes," he simply says, his shoulders dropping. His eyes tell me everything.

To be writing about grief so many years later is not painful but it is hard, because I belong to a club that I wish I didn't. If you live long enough you will lose people you love. Your grandparents might go first, then eventually your elderly parents, perhaps a colleague or friend will succumb to cancer, an acquaintance will die in a car crash abroad, your beloved pet will leave to run through the fields in the sky. Death touches all of us at some point along the way—it's in the natural order of things to lose people we love—but nothing had prepared me for the death of the man I had given my heart to. In the weeks after the funeral, I was shuttled between my mother's house and my sister's, to be looked after. The first morning I was on my own I typed the word "grief" into Google. Still in shock and not having eaten in days, I became the curious observer, wanting to know what I was dealing with—what were the symptoms of my impending illness and how could I cure it? I ordered ten books about grief that day and sat reading online definitions of the different stages: Denial—Anger—Bargaining—Depression—Acceptance. These five words seem so inadequate. I remember asking my therapist how long it would take me to "get better," to not cry on the bus, to sleep without the help of a bottle of wine. She said for some people it might take six months, while others may never get over it. Looking back, I'm grateful for her honesty. Some days I experienced all of the stages of grief at once, while other days I felt nothing at all, a complete void.

Grief is the brain's way of dealing with loss, and it is wretched. It took me a long time to understand that my love was no longer on the planet; he wasn't in another country, he wasn't at the office. He was erased off the face of the earth, permanently—my head could not accept it. Grief is like drowning; the tide pulls you under and the shock leaves you paralyzed. You sink down, lower and lower until you're lying on the seabed. You've given up the struggle; it's easier to lie there, drowning slowly. And then your survival instinct wakes up and you're suddenly kicking with all your might to pull away from the deadweight of the water, to save your own life. You kick to the surface and crash through into the air, gasping and spluttering, your lungs heaving. When you've calmed down, you remember he is dead, and your body goes limp as you slide back under the water, back down to the seabed. You don't *get over* grief—you move through it as you learn to live with the loss. You have to learn how to swim with it.

All and none of the books I bought during the first months were useful. I would read passages that brought tears of recognition, and seek out tales of loss in autobiographies, but found the detached tone many of the authors used left me feeling alone, their matter-of-fact explanations barely scraping the surface of how I felt. Often I found more comfort in novels, escaping into any story I could lay my hands on, the fastest way to get out of my head. It was around that time I discovered the headaches I'd been getting weren't just from the wine I was using to self-medicate; I needed reading glasses. Looking at my bespectacled reflection, all I could think was: "He'll never see me wear these." The smallest changes brought such pain.

Words were precious to me back then. I reread his cards and e-mails and returned to the bookshelf again and again to open books with his inscriptions inside. In the first year I wrote my pain out onto the page, filling my journals with letters to him, letters to myself, letters to the universe. I bargained, and raged, and remembered, and regretted, just as the books had said I would, a tsunami of emotion that flowed unfettered

and bloody, filling my throat and nose, drowning me. Days were lived minute-by-minute and it was a conscious act of will that kept me alive, that kept all the cells of my body sticking together. I felt I would simply disappear as he had done, if I didn't pay attention to every breath, every blink, every tiny movement. I only wanted to be with him, but it soon became very clear that there was no connecting flight to where he'd gone.

For months I watched the world and its inhabitants rush past me, a woman in a glass box, motionless, stilled. I envied my friends as they carried on with their routines: taking their kids to school, getting engaged, earning their living. I couldn't work for months. My family became increasingly worried as I sat at home all day, reading and writing, then staring into space until I noticed the room was dark, and even then I didn't bother to turn on the lights. When the pain downshifted into numbness, and my thoughts turned to ways out of the mess, some shrapnel of survival instinct must have kicked in, because I found myself in the doctor's office. I was seen by a woman doctor I hadn't met before, and when she gently suggested I needed some help to get through those days, I burst into tears. I felt relief. Yes, I needed help.

Those first six months were the hardest because the loss was so new, but every time period has its own flavor. As the weeks stretch into months you become convinced the pain will never end. Then as the ruminating and obsessing starts, your grief reaches new heights of tedium; you go over and over the smallest details of your loss, trying to remember everything you can, replaying conversations and arguments, and the last time they said they loved you. The bereaved measure time as if our life depended on it, gauging how far from the event we are in order to evaluate our progress. In the first year I was obsessed with time: two weeks, two months, six months, a year; all were reverently noted and memorialized. And then there was the waiting, the never-ending waiting for something that wasn't going to happen. If we are patient and grieve thoroughly and think every thought about our beloved, and wrestle with every unanswered question and feel the pain and anguish and hatred and sorrow and pop our pills and rant at our therapist and cry an ocean of tears and try to face up to the biggest most terrifying truth about life—death—*the deceased will still not come back to us*. There is no happy ending to bereavement, so we have to find a way to live with this knowledge and integrate it into our souls. But they don't come back. We have to learn to accept the unacceptable.

⤛

In many ways our love affair continued even after he was gone. Just because he wasn't there in body didn't mean he wasn't there in spirit, but it was my own mind that remade him every night, the dreams torturing me in their realness—he'd be there by my side, ethereal, insubstantial, but there. I'd be lying on the sofa and he'd be beside me running his hands down my back, whispering words against my skin that I'd forget the moment I woke up. So many mornings began with tears. It took a long time for the sensory memories to subside—I'd think I could smell him as I lay in bed, that I could feel him touching my arm; if I closed my eyes I could feel his lips on mine. I missed him in an acutely physical way, my body so used to the imprint of him inside me. I didn't know how to balance my yearning for him with my despair. It was maddening. In retrospect I understand why I drank so much, why I had to dull the aching to get some peace. I found it so hard to switch off, as if—were I to let go for a second, to take a break from the ever-vigilant awareness—I would fall down and dissolve. So I sat at my desk every day, coiled like a spring, perched on the seat, waiting. At times I'd purposely make it hurt more by playing songs that reminded me of him, silly lyrics we'd sung together in the car. I'd open a bottle of wine, listening to the music, and drink and drink until I had to crawl to my bedroom and get into bed.

His heart attack had been so swift and sudden I hadn't been able to say good-bye, so the unanswered questions haunted me. It's the unending silence that sends the bereaved to psychics,

seeking one more chance to say the things you wanted to say out loud, looking for their consoling words. I wanted to believe I could speak to him again, that a stranger could open her mouth and his words would fall out. There were many candle-lit nights when I tried to feel closer to where he was. It was hard to maintain any faith in an afterlife when the silence was so deafening, but living so intimately with death can play tricks with your mind. I convinced myself that if I just sat still for long enough, if I just thought about him *hard enough*, he would come back.

There wasn't any particular moment when my healing began, but moving back to the coast gave me the head and heart space I needed. I've never regretted leaving London the way I did. It also meant I was closer to my oldest friend. There were many evenings when helping Madeleine make dinner for the kids was the most soothing balm I could have wished for, the constant noise and chatter bringing me back into my body and aware of what day it was. Children are so alive, so in the *right now*, like little Zen masters in Spiderman pajamas.

I was chopping a red pepper when I felt a tug on my sleeve and looked down to see eight-year-old Oscar standing beside me.

"Did your boyfriend die?" he asked, his face open like a bloom. I crouched down on my heels and looked him in the eye, trying to smile reassuringly.

"Yes he did," I said. Oscar looked uncertain for a moment. "Does it make you sad?"

"Yes it does," I said, "but it's okay to feel sad. It just means I miss him."

"I'm sorry you feel sad," he said, and then threw his arms around my neck, squeezing me hard. His hair smelled of sea air and soap. Then, as quickly as he came in, he ran out of the kitchen. It was moments like these, punctuating my days alone, that helped me to taste life again.

Each person experiences grief in their own individual way. And though I have often thought that to lose a child would be the most devastating loss of all, there is no hierarchy to grief—only we can know the pain we feel and what we have lost. Death is brutal and final but there are other losses we will grieve for: divorce, redundancy, infertility, natural disasters. To assimilate the loss—to make sense of the change—we must allow ourselves to fully inhabit the pain for as long as we need to. In my case I collapsed into my bereavement, such was the nature of the loss I felt. I gave up living normally for a while; I had to let myself wallow and suffocate and drown in the emotion to be able to get through it. The healing began slowly—making it to the corner shop without crying, or reading the newspaper and connecting with the outside world, remembering that I was a part of it too. Whenever I spent the afternoon with my godchildren and found myself laughing as I pushed them on the swings, down on my knees making sandcastles, I was living back in the present. Those afternoons were rare at first, and every time I'd be filled with remorse for having forgotten about him for an hour or two—how could I? But life is tricky in how it pulls you toward the light. The antidepressants were helping me climb back to the surface, and my weekly therapy appointments gave me space to go back over the ground, again and again, uncovering every grievance, every bad word, every regret. I'd had a few sessions with a bereavement counselor when I'd first moved away, but it soon became clear that working with a psychotherapist was what I needed. There was so much to unravel.

The circumstances of the death can have a huge impact on the way you grieve. Had I been able to say good-bye, had I known it was coming, perhaps it would have been a little easier, though even writing that makes me shake my head—there's no way to make death easier to accept. Ours was not the greatest love that ever existed. There were fights and breakups, jealousy and disappointments. It was a flawed, very human love that burned furiously for two whole years. It was passionate and obsessive, and with the benefit of hindsight, I might not have made the same choices—six years after he died, I am at peace with that last sentence. It does not betray what we had, it simply

After so much vigilance, after
all that waiting, the first
anniversary—a day I thought
would be so achingly significant—
was just another day. Nothing had
changed; everything remained the
same. He was still gone.

recognizes that I am no longer that thirty-year-old woman who fell in love with a man with twinkly blue eyes. Yet, when he died all our problems died with him, leaving only the love behind. Our relationship ended in the middle of the conversation, and there was still so much to say. I have often regretted not saying *I love you* more. Not kissing him more—who cares about all those future plans when I once had him standing in front of me? Regrets are never easy to bear. If I had our time again there's so much I would do differently.

At first I could not bear to look at photographs of him, trapped on pieces of paper, but as the first anniversary of his death approached, I found myself wanting to have his picture around my home, wanting him to share my space now that I was feeling more in control. When the actual day arrived I caught a matinee in town, needing to do something mundane to get me through the twenty-four hours. As I ate dinner that night I drank a toast in his honor and put myself to bed early—not a tear had been shed. The next day was very different. I walked to my therapist's house unable to stop crying. Sitting down on the sofa opposite her, I looked up and said, "He didn't come back." After so much vigilance, after all that waiting, the first anniversary—a day I thought would be so achingly significant—was just another day. Nothing had changed; everything remained the same. He was still gone.

There comes a time when we must divorce the dead, when we must end the relationship in our own way. For me, it was a gradual process of letting go that started the day I packed away the mementos I had around my home. Twenty months after he died I returned to London to see a friend; it wasn't the first time I'd been back to the city, but it was the first time I'd felt ready to revisit my old address. It was a sunny Wednesday morning when I walked along that street, looking up at the windows of my former home, wondering who was living there now. Being there wasn't as upsetting as I'd feared it would be, and even as a thousand memories washed over me, I felt calm, acknowledging how far I had come. Walking farther down Westbourne Grove I stopped for lunch at my favorite spot, and as I sat in the sunshine I realized the grief that had anchored me for so long had shifted. I wasn't sure who I was without the loss defining me, but I knew the air had changed; that I was laughing more and making plans for work. That I could talk about what happened without tears taking over. That I really had survived.

When I returned home the next day I took an early evening walk on the beach. For the first time in a very long time, I allowed myself to imagine what it would be like to be held in another's arms again. I had always pushed these thoughts down, but that night they danced around me, tempting me with whispers, and once they were out I couldn't squash them back inside. And there was a part of me that didn't want to, because it went far beyond the desire for a partner—I felt life calling to me. The energy of the city had filled me up, and I could see myself living there again, one day.

⟶

Grief doesn't just get up and leave you alone. There will always be sadness attached to his death, but six years later I am able to look back on our years together with fondness. I still have conversations with him in my head and have yet to form a new relationship with another man, but that doesn't mean I am holding on to him. I learned how to live with the loss, and then I learned how to live my life again. His death set me on a path I never imagined I would take; it took years to find my feet again, but once I did the healing began in earnest. There were many gifts in our relationship, but it's my relationship with him since he passed that has brought the most treasures. I never thought that could be possible, but it is true.

His death has taught me how to empathize with others' distress. I learned how to sit with my own pain and breathe my way through it. I learned how to uncover all the grievances I had held so close to me and pick them apart to heal them, and let them go. I unraveled all the knots in my past, and I started weaving a new story, one that has the real me at the heart of it, not my neediness or my shame or my insecurity. I found myself, and I learned to love the less-than-perfect bits, of which there are many. I opened myself to my creativity again and discovered that the words and images had been inside me all along, just waiting for their day in the sunshine. I followed my newly mended heart and found a way to support myself doing work that excites me and helps others—that has been such a gift. And I know he'd be proud of me.

In the beginning I couldn't understand why he died—it was so sudden and shocking, I simply couldn't accept it; and yet here I am, with all that is around me and all that is ahead of me, and I can't help feeling it was supposed to be this way. I have integrated his death into my own life. I have healed and moved forward, inch by inch, until I am now far enough away to find gratitude for the journey I've been on. The journey that continues until he and I meet again.

Even though each of us finds our own unique path through grief, there are four touchstones I want to share, in case you ever find yourself in the maelstrom of longing and need a hand to hold.

The first is a gentle reminder to feel your pain.

It's human nature to want to protect ourselves from pain at all costs, but grief doesn't give us a chance to duck and avoid the blow. It consumes us and then spits us back out, burning through our old life to make room for the new reality. We feel the pain because we loved them, because we miss them, because we want them back; but it's possible to get trapped in the denial, to reject what happened, to put on a brave face for others and say we're doing fine. We can push the pain away, but it will be waiting for us. If we truly desire to feel whole again, to be able to find meaning in our lives once more, we must feel our pain, so we can eventually let it go.

The second reminder is to find support.

At first my family and friends rallied around me, listening, loving, supporting me as best they could, but as the months passed I sank farther into my own world. The alone felt safe and I let myself fall, but finding a therapist proved to be the best and bravest thing I have ever done. It didn't feel like that at first; it took me twenty-four hours to build up to leaving the house for the first appointment. But having permission to talk helped me process my chaotic thoughts and start making sense of what had happened. My loved ones listened and consoled, but it was the impartial, consistent presence of my therapist, Jill, that cut through the depression, sending out a lifeline that brought me back to shore.

The third reminder is to pay attention,

because somewhere in all the muck are the clues to help you find the way back to your life. As we learn to live with the loss, we find new ways to live in the world, and what was once important may look very different to us now. Being so well acquainted with death brings with it a new appreciation for life, and over time we may feel a renewed sense of purpose that has never been there before. It might be your children, your community, a charity, or the work you share with the world, but somewhere within the healing and recovery is a way to imbue our lives with new meaning. It's a hidden gift of bereavement, one we could never have imagined existed at the beginning, but it's there nonetheless. It may take years, but we do come back to the world, I promise we do.

The final reminder is the reassurance that time will help.

Time in itself does not heal pain, it just moves us farther and farther away from the one we lost. But the grief does get easier to bear and you will find ways to cope. This was what I so desperately needed to hear in the first months. I didn't believe it, of course, but I share it with you now because it *did* get easier. I *did* cope. I *did* survive. And I want you to know. Even if you don't believe it today, tuck these reminders away in a drawer, so you know where to find them should you ever need them.

We do not choose grief, but in many ways it is the most extraordinary journey we will ever take. And I hate that I know this now—that I know how I will feel again one day, when another person I love shoves off their mortal coil and leaves me behind. But how else do we know we are alive unless we know death? It is six years since I last looked into his eyes. I am living a life that I've built and nurtured, and he is not here to see it, and I accept that. I no longer muse on the could-have-beens and the would-have-dones; instead, I honor him every day that I live my life by my own rules and follow my heart. When I share what I know, and pass on the lessons his death taught me, I celebrate the time we had together. Words and dreams have been born out of this grief, and I am grateful to the man who gave me this gift, purely because he stepped out into the light before I did.

We do survive. And then we thrive.

reflection

It took me a long time to stop obsessing over what I would have
said to him had I known he was going to die. After I moved to
Bath and began feeling more settled, I found the letting go came
quite naturally to me, as my thoughts turned toward the future
and what I wanted to achieve, rather than the past and what I'd
lost. My love became a cherished friend, one who was now far
away, and I felt at peace with that. I kept a photo of him in a frame
on my sideboard, a comforting presence as I adjusted to life in
a new city. Then one evening, a few months in, I felt inspired to
light a candle and sit with his photo, taking it out of the frame
and holding it in my hands. Looking at his face no longer made
me sad; I felt warmth and love, and an overwhelming sense of
gratitude. Taking my journal, I began to write a last letter to him,
thanking him for the years we'd shared and telling him the story
of what I'd learned since he left. And when I stopped writing I
found I didn't want to put his photo back in the frame—instead
I tucked it into my journal, closed my eyes, and let him go. Four
years after he'd died, I truly felt the release, and it was gentle and
right.

   We never know when loss will sweep into our lives, and
while we're doing our best to make ends meet, it's easy to let
the important things remain unsaid.

Taking a new page in your journal, draw up a list of all the people who matter to you: family and friends, teachers and mentors, neighbors and colleagues. Who are the people on your team? Who inspires you to be your best self?

Starting with the first person on your list, write down all the ways he or she makes your life better. Think about the good times you've shared, the significant days, the memories you don't want to forget. Keep writing—note form is perfect for this—until you're filled with all the good feelings you have for that person. Next, do something to reach out to them. You could . . .

> . . . make a phone call;
>
> . . . handwrite a letter;
>
> . . . type a quick e-mail;
>
> . . . send a "thinking of you" postcard;
>
> . . . or hide a note in their lunchbox.

Make a regular date with yourself to continue working through your list in this way, one person each day or week. If there are loved ones on your list who are no longer here, write them a letter and read it out loud.

Tell them what they mean to you. Start today.

the tides

"The cure for anything is saltwater; sweat, tears or the sea."

—ISAK DINESEN

When I need perspective, when hormones or stress
or whatever it is that's making me suffer is closing
in, a voice in my head urges: *Go outside.* I've often wondered
if having a garden would make me a saner person, being able
to stand on the earth whenever I wanted, just by opening a
door—imagine the novelty! As it is I have to find shoes, descend
five flights of stairs, and walk along streets until I arrive at the
nearest park; then I can plant my feet on the grass, sit under
the magnolia trees when they bloom in the spring, or enjoy the
shade in the summer, the russet leaves in the autumn, the bare
branches at the end and beginning of every year. And it feels
good to be there, walking through nature, even if it is main-
tained by human hands. But still I hear the voice, quieter now,
a little forlorn:

I miss the sea.

I grew up by the coast with sand between my toes and sun-
burnt shoulders soothed with calamine lotion. We lived in a
town where people took their summer vacation so we didn't
have to travel to get to a beach—it was always there. Perhaps we
took it for granted at times, but the smell of the sea has been
the smell of home all my life. I've walked along the seafront
as a child and an adult; past the arcade games and the fish 'n'

chip shops, the beach huts with the public showers at the end, where I'd rinse the sand off my feet before traipsing back to the car, the path too steep, my sandals rubbing as my mother called back, telling me to hurry up.

When he died I knew I had to go back to the sea, to be near the tides that were calling me home. Those first few months were raw and bloody, but the waves took me out of myself, the constant motion kneading me back to the present moment, a reprieve from the keening. When I could find it in me to pull on my clothes and leave the house I'd walk down to the beach, journal in hand, and sit on a cafe terrace, writing out my thoughts until my hand ached. What would start as anger and confusion was soon lulled by the sound of the waves breaking, every stubborn thought I tackled left wilting on the page, as I wrote further and deeper into how I was feeling. I waited for the day to arrive when I would run onto the sand and scream my loss into the wind, but it never came—the breeze that blew over me cosseted me, cotton wool against my cheeks. I always felt taken care of and it was easier to assimilate what had happened when I was away from my tear-soaked pillows. Being alone at home was the problem.

In the autumn I'd walk for miles, passing the occasional dog walker, more than content to just be with myself, picking up shells and putting them in my pockets. I'd walk as far as the beach huts painted red and yellow, past the last of the tourists, their kids digging holes in the sand, hair plastered to their faces. Looking out to the horizon I'd fancy I could see the curve of the planet, that if I stood really still I'd feel the movement, the turning reminding me I couldn't go backwards. And then there was my bench, the one by the blue hut, where I'd sit for hours, reading or writing, watching the seagulls scuttle along the promenade, pecking at scraps before swooping back into the air. I was joined once by an old woman, her head wrapped in a silk scarf, running shoes on her feet. With one hand on her walking stick she shut her eyes, setting her mouth in a determined line as she sat like the queen of the beach, letting the wind wash over her. I was too shy to say hello, but I smiled as I left and she nodded her head before closing her eyes against the wind again, regal and quietly composed. I wondered if she had a husband waiting at home, or was she like me, grieving the loss of a beloved. My thoughts turned to my paternal grandmother, who'd lived for three more years after Granddad passed on. How she sat alone in that house waiting for visits from us; how she'd had to learn how to reset the clock and manage the bills. I phoned her every Sunday from the city, and we'd talk about my job and plans, and she'd tell me about her week. When we talked about Granddad she'd give a little sob and I never really knew what to say, except "I love you, Gran."

She always replied, "Well, you know I love you," and then she'd tell me to *go gently* and we'd hang up the phone. Walking back from the beach that day I wished I'd visited her more in those last years, now that I knew the endlessly silent days of grieving. My heart ached to think of her sitting alone in her house.

The sea air always brought new perspectives with it, creeping in through the gaps in the windows of my home, whirling around me, invisible and stealthy, collecting the dislodged fragments of my self, and helping my shattered heart knit back together again. I walked on the beach as often as I could, as often as my grief would allow me. There were many days when getting out of bed was not a possibility.

I've faced the Pacific and Atlantic Oceans, the Mediterranean and Caribbean Seas, but the coastline that edges the English Channel is the one I call home—familiar and safe, a sanctuary filled with so many memories they cancel each other out, creating a neutral space I can inhabit without the tang of other heartaches getting in the way. Joseph Campbell said, "Your sacred space is where you can find yourself again and again." I think we all need a sanctuary, a sacred place that reconnects us to ourselves and gives us courage when our supplies are drying up. A place where we can commune with something greater than ourselves, in small quiet moments of reflection, or in the outward majesty that takes our breath away. It might be a place that's shared with thousands of others; it might be a space you've made all your own. The ocean, a forest, a lake, your own garden—the natural world resets our brains back to the earthly rhythm of tides and seasons, growth and hibernation. When I sink too far into my head, nature reminds me I'm just worm food, that the leaves will fall no matter what I do, and the tides will never stop churning the ocean; it has always been so. Even during the worst of the pain, I was able to gain a little perspective—momentarily, at least—by venturing outside my home, and myself, for a while. I have days when my heart aches for the sea, and I wonder, again, why I now live in a landlocked city so far from the shore, promising myself that I'll go visit the sea, that a two-hour drive is better than a four-hour plane ride. I live in a country surrounded by water, after all, how hard can it be?

I've always hoped that there's something more to this world than the things I see in front of me, something beyond the wars and taxes and the shriveled apple sitting in my fruit bowl. I'm not a religious person, but I'm often impressed by the devout faith of those able to believe in something so wholeheartedly. This has never been my way; even as a young child I wanted to figure it out for myself. Other than the hymns we sang at school I had a secular upbringing and wasn't forced to go to Sunday School like so many of my friends. I did briefly belong to a church choir because my music teacher suggested I go along, and, ever the enterprising ten-year-old, I joined because they paid me—pennies really, but worth it to me. We earned more for weddings and christenings, and those brown envelopes filled with coins were my very first earnings, quickly exchanged for notebooks and pens.

Despite my lack of religious fervor, there is a place for the sacred in my world. My reverence for books borders on fanatical, and then there's the unconscious altar making, arranging treasured objects next to bowls filled with pebbles and shells. Burning incense and candles has been an evening ritual for as long as I can remember. Twenty years ago I tried to pry open the doors in my mind with dance music and a chemical crowbar. These days a tuberose-scented candle will suffice—how times have changed. I'm not a Christian, yet I feel so peaceful listening to choir practice on a Saturday afternoon in Bath Abbey; I'm not a Buddhist, yet there are mala beads and a Buddha statue sitting on my coffee table. They're pretty and decorative, but more than that, they're borrowed symbols that represent the reflective space I wish to cultivate in my life. I don't want anyone to tell me the answers, but like a spiritual

magpie I gather the gems that catch my eye and assemble a way
to exist in the world that feels meaningful to me.

The older I get the more I desire a deeper connection to my
true self, my family, and the places in the world that feel like
home. Navigating my way through grief, and the healing that
followed, removed all the bullshit from my life. Where I lost
friends I gained soul mates, where I'd clung to job titles I found
my true calling, and where I was skeptical I found tantalizing
hints of what felt like proof. Even writing that makes me nervous, but here's the truth: You can't go through an experience
like the death of a loved one and not come out the other side
with opinions about what happens after we die. There were
many nights I sat in the darkness and willed him to reappear,
when I would have given anything for just one more kiss. It
took a long time to come to terms with the physicality of death,
that the body stops working and has to be disposed of—in his
case, cremation. I wanted to know why his body couldn't be
reanimated, why I couldn't keep him in bed with me. There's
no logic in grief, just yearning and missing.

And then there were the feathers.

About six months after his death I sat in the conserva-
tory of my therapist's home, our regular Tuesday session. The
sun was streaming in through the glass roof, but I didn't feel
the heat on my skin. The night before I'd read about a woman

whose husband had been killed in a helicopter crash. I'd been sifting through the words to find some comfort. How did she survive her loss? How do I do this? She said she still sensed her husband's presence, that strange things would happen letting her know he was looking after her. Once, a few years after his death, she was sitting on her sofa at home when she looked up and saw a feather floating down from the ceiling. No window was open and she couldn't fathom where the feather had come from, but she said she knew it was a gift from her husband. Several years later she went back to the place where his helicopter had crashed and wrote very movingly about how she heard a voice whispering quietly in her ear, and she knew, without a doubt, that it was him. He had urged her to write the book I had in my hands that evening.

"She had all those amazing signs and I have nothing," I told my therapist. "It's like he's just disappeared and forgotten me. I'm not getting any messages from the grave. There's just nothing!"

Jill patiently listened to my tearful ranting and by the end of our hour I felt a little calmer as I said good-bye. Usually I'd walk home along the busy roads, but that afternoon I decided to head to the sea. The tears had left me raw and I couldn't face going home, yet again, to an empty flat; I needed to be outside for a while longer. At the bottom of the road was a path that wove through the wood leading down to the sea front. I hadn't

walked this way before, and needing to pay attention to where I was going helped to keep my head clear. As I stepped on the path I saw a small white feather in front of me. A few steps later I saw another . . . then another . . . then another. By now I was smiling. In the ten minutes it took to walk to the beach I saw literally hundreds of feathers, the path strewn like a fairy-tale carpet. Looking around at the trees, I felt the air buzzing, a sparkly energy that made me feel light-headed. By the time I walked back out into the sunlight I felt wrapped in my lover's playful arms, grateful tears flowing unabashed. A fifteen-minute walk along the beach took me to another wood, the one that led to my road. I didn't see a single feather on that path, not even one.

From then on feathers were the way I knew he was near me—I'd be thinking about him in the street, and the next moment a feather would appear on my path. I'd find them in the house—little white ones between the pages of my books, a gray feather in the bathroom. It was strange and comforting, and comfort is so welcome when you're trapped in the twilight between life and death. I remember reading somewhere that the bereaved often report feeling the presence of their loved one in the first year; the rational part of me wants to believe it's just the shock that makes us fantasize and project, that we'd believe anything to feel closer to the one we lost. But there comes a point when the seeming coincidences happen so often you can't help but wonder. Believing it was him got me through the days. It was something to hold on to when I was falling down.

Breaking out of my daily routine once in a while helps me appreciate this life I have. When we survive a traumatic event or transition in our lives, there's a point when the healing really starts to take hold and we suddenly feel invincible. I often found myself standing at the cheese counter in the grocery store wanting to yell, "I'm still alive!" Even the most mundane moments seemed heroic achievements after so many months of inertia. Soon enough, the euphoria of surviving wears off and we return to the ordinariness of our day-to-day lives. Years later, I miss the gratitude I felt for another day in front of me to breathe in and exhale, so for a fast-track back to that feeling I take a trip somewhere new. It's impossible to ignore your aliveness when walking down a new street in a new town or new country. As I get older I find I have a better appreciation for dear old England, the land that will always be home. But as I stretch these newfound wings I yearn to catch an updraft and fly farther than I have before.

Travel is sacred to me. It's mind-numbingly boring at times; it's tiring and stressful and often expensive, but it expands my inner world like nothing else. I've never been one for backpacks and tents. As a young woman I was too scared and too broke to travel alone. Falling in love with an Italian set me up for a decade of trips to Italy—always going back to his hometown, always seeing the same people, always coming home laden with *parmigiano* and *prosciutto crudo* and the guilt his mother tucked into our suitcases. For an English girl whose only experience abroad was a week in Spain in 1983, spending two weeks with his family was beyond intimidating. I was grateful for the friends that spoke a little English, but most of the time I was smiling and mute. Unable to follow conversations my mind would drift off, always *la ragazza inglese* with the pale skin, sheltering under the beach umbrella, nose in a book while the rest of them talked—everyone had an opinion and they shared it vociferously.

Now I love to travel alone. I get the most exquisite thrill as I check my bags and make my way through security to find my gate. Having only ever flown once as a child, international travel still feels glamorous to me, and I appreciate the anonymity that airports provide, the space to narrate my own adventure. Though I try very hard not to, I usually overpack, but my carry-on bag is always the same: notebook and pen, several books, moisturizer, eye drops, and a shawl. With these small comforts at my feet, my seat is transformed into sacred space, and for the next five or ten hours I give myself over to the journey, reading, journaling, sleeping if I can. To close my eyes in England and open them again in Kenya, Cairo, Jamaica, Boston . . . I can think of no better definition of magic.

Traveling with a partner or friend is very different from traveling on your own. I love the freedom of going solo, not having to tie myself down to another's schedule. I'm a selfish traveler. When I'm in a new city I gulp down everything I see, taking photographs constantly—of the sidewalk and the graffiti, the decayed and the different. I try to hide my camera when I'm not using it, wanting to blend in with the locals and feel a part of the city's current. I want to soak in the tastes and sounds, and have the new and the strange rub off on my skin so I take more than photographs home with me. My first day in San Francisco I walked across the city from Japantown down to Crissy Field, following my nose, glancing at the map in my bag once or twice, but finding my way quite easily without it. I stopped at a restaurant along the way for urgent refueling, and when I reached the ocean my jet-lagged body relaxed as the salt air wrapped around me. A stranger in a place I'd never been before, yet so curiously at home. I sat on the sand, looking out across to the Golden Gate Bridge, and then opened my journal.

"Something has shifted," I wrote. "I feel more open, and coming to San Francisco represents my new openness to life, my willingness to take a chance, to do something that scares me and see what happens."

My second day in Marrakesh we hired a guide to take us through the souks. The first day had been chaotic as we got lost on our way back to our riad, four pale women beaten down by the sun. So on day two we wised up and got help. Aziz was our man, a chef and tour guide who told us about his daughter who was studying in England. He knew all the souk sellers by name, of course, and took us through the alleys packed with metalsmiths and leather workshops, the pungent smell of cowhides a challenge first thing in the morning. After haggling for ornate silver trays and kaftans, we landed at a souk with walls covered in jewel-colored *babouches*. With so much choice there was only one thing for it: try on as many slippers as we could.

Worried we were taking too long, I went to look for Aziz and found him sitting on a stool at the entrance, sipping mint tea and holding court with the neighboring sellers. He looked up at me and smiled. "Please, take your time!"

"Are you sure? I promise we won't be much longer."

"It is not a problem. I always say: People in a hurry are already dead."

And with that he shooed me back inside.

It was a treat meeting Aziz, the affable man about town who knew everyone and seemed to be liked by everyone too. No doubt he'd ushered hundreds of tourists just like us through the medina, but I appreciated our intelligent conversation, and his words have stuck with me ever since: *People in a hurry are already dead.* You can't hurry in Morocco in July, it's just too damn hot. You can't hurry through your life, it's just too damn short.

Three months later I had a breakfast meeting in New York City with my editor and agent, and I left feeling invincible and excited. I wandered through Madison Square Park and carried on toward Bleeker Street and into Greenwich Village. Everything felt different and yet familiar. After a lifetime of watching films set in this city, the mythology of the place had seeped into my consciousness. Snapping my way through the kaleidoscope of restaurants, I found a bookshop with a poster of Patti Smith and Robert Mapplethorpe displayed in the window. Lured inside—who can resist a new bookshop?— I browsed for an hour, thumbing books about the city and books about writing, and poetry and biographies and anything else that caught my eye, the covers like cupcakes waiting

to be unwrapped. Walking back out into the sunshine I set off in what felt like the right direction, letting my feet lead the way with no particular agenda. I turned a corner and found myself facing a street painted with dappled light through the trees, pockets of sunshine glowing golden bright, the scent of garlic and burnt sugar mixing with the hot and dirty sidewalk. For a moment I was dazzled—the scene seemed almost other-worldly—and in that moment I felt more connected to him, and more connected to possibility, than ever. We'd always planned to visit New York together, and standing on that street I truly felt his presence. Taking one last deep breath I snapped a single shot of the street and said "Thank you" out loud, tucking the moment into my heart to bring home with me. And then I carried on walking.

Travel teaches me self-respect. Away from the numbing routines I use to keep the frustrations at bay, I am left with myself. I can't avoid my wants and needs—set to a fresh new backdrop, the familiar stripped away. Sacred moments are easier to find when we're away from home, our senses alert, our eyes wide open as we explore places we've never seen before. But this connection to our surroundings can be channeled back home too, when we take our children to school and linger a little longer in the sunshine; when we get in the car and drive for an hour, just for the hell of it. Life is a collection of single moments strung together with the continuity of our hopes and experiences, our memories the glue that keeps it all together.

Close your eyes and take a moment. Can you feel it? Your aliveness?

People in a hurry are already dead.

reflection

Not every day will be sacred. When the car breaks down and the baby's teething and we're cut to the core with self-loathing and despair . . . No, not every day is a party, but this just makes the party days all the sweeter. Eking out little pockets of sacred space in our day helps ease us through every twenty-four hours. For me, a really stellar cup of coffee made with freshly ground beans creates a small oasis in my working day. I like the ritual of the grinding and the brewing and always using my favorite mug. It's a very simple pleasure but it makes me feel cared for as I savor every sip.

In *The Sea, The Sea*, Iris Murdoch's protagonist said: "The secret to a happy life is continuous small treats." I feel the truth of this statement all the way down to the roots of my being. Having something to look forward to is a potent motivator; the promise of a reward has convinced generations of children to clean their rooms. We grown-ups are not that different.

Spend the next half hour making a list of all the small treats that bring you joy. Write down the foods you love to eat, the places you like to visit, the sounds you love to hear, and the things that make you feel good. Foot rubs and hot scented baths. Sushi. Sitting under a tree. Fresh flowers. Charlotte

Brontë novels. Mojitos. *The Sound of Music*. Playing with your neighbor's dog. Whatever it is, write it down.

When you have a list of at least twenty small treats, take a pack of index cards and write out one treat per card. If you're feeling particularly crafty, you could decorate your cards with paint and collage, or even photograph your small treats and use the prints as cards—Polaroids would be perfect for this. Keep your cards in a box or basket, somewhere where they'll catch your eye. Add more cards to your box as new treats occur to you.

Then once a week—or preferably more—select a card at random from the box and *treat yourself.* No excuses, no apologies—

enjoy your treat, knowing you deserve it.

redrafting the blueprint

"Memories of the past are not memories of facts but memories of your imaginings of the facts."

—Philip Roth

I am perched on a rock facing the sea, the wind blowing my hair into my face, the paper cup of coffee in my hands threatening to burn my fingers. I have a camera full of images in my bag, and the colors of the beach huts and sky have soothed my grief-heavy mind. I feel comfortable in my solitude; the calm sea reflects my mood and I'm pleased I made the effort to get out of the house. A little girl with blonde hair as fine as cobwebs sits down on the rock beside me. She takes off her shoes and socks, neatly places them on the sand between us, then tip-toes over the shells out onto the main swath of beach, a red kite in tow. I watch as she struggles to untangle the strings. "Dad!" she shouts against the wind, and a dark-haired man walks over to her and patiently prepares the kite for flight. This takes five minutes or so, and as I watch I feel a sudden sadness. Their life of kites and grazed knees feels so far away from where I am right now. It's a scene from a possible future, but underneath this reverie is an older ache.

On the ride home I think about another beach, a lifetime ago. It was a chilly autumn day, and my sister and I were digging in the sand. Suddenly, seemingly out of nowhere, a Labrador raced up to my sister, barking excitedly, making her jump backwards, shrieking. In one smooth movement my father scooped her up and shouted "No!" at the dog. My sister looked so small in his arms, and I remember the sound of her

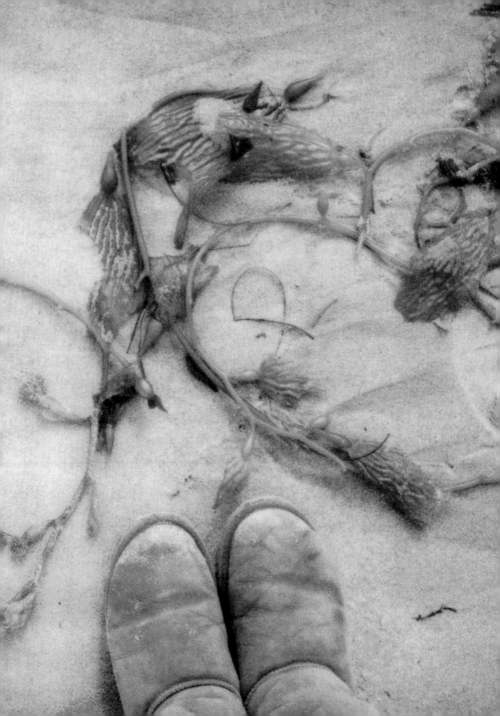

crying without pausing for breath like she was never going to stop. I don't remember what I did or whether the dog came for me—all I saw was my frightened sister, all I felt was the tightness in my throat. We gathered the buckets and shovels and headed back to the car. My father carried her all the way.

If you were able to rewrite your memories, would you want to? Not all of them—just the ones that catch your insides, scratching and scraping like a ripped nail. I can tell you other stories from my childhood, and while they may or may not be wholly accurate they are the stories I carry with me and the ones that float to the surface when I close my eyes and try to remember. What if we retell our stories, and in the retelling the new tale becomes the truth? The past is just the soil we grew up in, a blueprint we can redraft if we look at it from another perspective. But where to start? Two milestones mark my path: my father walking out the door and the death of the man I loved, two decades later. Yet the smaller dips in the road, the rest stops and detours, offer as much illumination as the big life-altering crashes. Every corner turned is a story waiting to happen.

When we're young we race through life, anxious to have all the benefits we think adult status will bring. Yet here we are, all grown up, and suddenly life's getting shorter, a breathless race from first coffee of the morning to teeth brushing before bed. What really happens in the minutes in between? There are pieces I wish to remember, the moments of seeming inconsequence I can relive when all is quiet and I take a memory out to examine its shape and texture. My picture-taking compulsion is born out of this desire to remember. I have a box full of photographs dating back through the decades of my life. Some have curled edges, their shiny sides yellowing and cracked; most have dates written on the back, and I recognize my grandmother's handwriting, my mother's, my own. I have watery memories attached to these photos: I remember that my parents took me to the zoo because the photos tell me I was there. Alas, no one had a camera out for my very first kiss; I keep such tender memories carefully stored in files in my head.

I think photographs anchor us in our lives, giving us something from the past to hold on to so we're not spinning off into space. As a photographer I know how to layer meaning through my images, how the choice of camera and subject matter conspire to evoke a response in the viewer. But the photographs from my childhood weren't taken with such ends in mind; I know it's the emotion and meaning I attach to them that gives them their true power. I don't take them for granted; they are clues to my life that grow ever more poignant as time passes.

One photo makes me pause: my father looking straight into the camera lens with tired eyes, his curling beard almost touching the baby in his arms. I am only a few weeks old, with wide blue eyes and no idea what the years will bring me. I sense the look on his face is the one most new fathers wear and I can tell in that moment he took his new role seriously, carefully holding his firstborn. In another photo he holds me up against a clear summer sky, his bare shoulders tanned, and he's smiling at me. The size of my father's sideburns tells me it's the 1970s. Looking more closely I notice I've inherited his hands: long slender fingers, neat nails, rather feminine for a man of his height and build. I've been seeing myself in him a lot recently as I catch up to his age in the last of the photos, the photographic records ending abruptly when he left the country for good. I was just eleven years old. I've seen him four or five times in the intervening years, but I do not know him. As I write these words emotions bubble up in my chest and I wonder if I will ever truly feel at peace with what happened. As an adult I understand how flawed and fallible we all are, and how becoming a parent doesn't make you invulnerable to making mistakes. I see how the screw-ups of past generations are passed down to each of us, and how we do the best we can with the tools we have. I see how not everybody is cut out for parenthood. But as I near the age he was when he left, I still wonder how he was able to turn his back on his daughters so easily, choosing to leave the country with another woman and make a new family on the other side of the world.

Both my parents were born at the tail end of the Second World War and from the snippets of stories I've gleaned over the years it's clear that neither had the happiest childhoods. Victorian values informed so much of my mother's upbringing—my grandmother made her share her bed when she was *unwell* each month. My paternal grandfather was a strict man and the rifts that formed in my father's family later on tell me that despite the best efforts of my grandmother, my father's youth must have been difficult too. He left school to join the police force in London where he met my mother at an office dance. They married in 1963 and ten years later I was born. We could all spend a lifetime unraveling the knots of our childhood, but at some point you realize the knots are no longer yours. They belong to your parents, and their parents before them. The legacy is long and complicated, the damage passed on through generations, until one day someone finally stops and says: *This story does not belong to me.*

So many of my ideas about my young self were based on what I'd been told rather than my own experience. "You're just like your father" doesn't sit so well when you're confused about your feelings toward the man who left you. I carried a particular story about him for a long time: the moody guy who read science fiction books and had to be reminded to take a bath. *How am I like him?* Even now I struggle to find many good memories floating in a sea of uncomfortable silences and disappointments. I remember overhearing an argument from behind the kitchen door, holding my breath to stop myself from screaming. The sound of my parents' shouts made me suddenly need the toilet. Later, as we rode into town, my mother turned to me and said, "I'm sorry you had to hear that today." I didn't know what to say. I wasn't used to her speaking to me in this way. I felt uncomfortable and shy, as if she was telling me a secret I didn't want to know. Now I can imagine how hard it must have been: her marriage ending, her husband wanting out, and her self-esteem crumbling in the face of his infidelities. I haven't forgiven my father yet. I've tried to—I know it will be for my benefit, not his; that it will release the pain and open a space in my heart—but the forgiveness just doesn't come.

Perhaps I missed an opportunity eleven years ago when my mother received a letter from my father, telling us he was coming to England and asking if we'd be willing to meet him. The ostensible reason for his return was my grandfather's ailing health, but his letter made us wonder if perhaps he was finally ready to face the familial music. I wasn't sure I wanted to spend time with him, but I couldn't deny my curiosity about the shadowy man who'd influenced so much of my life. We arranged to meet with a series of achingly polite e-mails between England and Australia.

I don't think I've ever been as nervous as I was that morning. We had no idea how to greet him. "I don't think I can hug him," my sister said. I had to agree—the man was a stranger to us. It all felt horribly surreal. It was Abby who spotted him first: a rather haggard-looking man walking along the street, his mustache now gray, his hair barely there. When we stood up to greet him he came over and hugged us so fast we couldn't offer our hands instead. He ordered a drink from the waitress with more bravado than was necessary, evidently as nervous as we were. The polite conversation I'd anticipated didn't last long as he stumbled over our names and launched into what he needed to say. He spoke of the decision to leave our lives, a decision he thought was correct at the time, but with hindsight knew was wrong. He said it had hurt him that we hadn't stayed in touch, to which I felt obliged to point out that it wasn't our responsibility to do so—he was the parent, after all, and we had been so young. With more calmness than I felt, I told him how his actions had affected us, tried to explain how his leaving had damaged us, how we hadn't understood. I knew Abby didn't know what to say, so I spoke for us both, gathering all my twenty-eight-year-old wits about me. But I felt like a child, lacking the right words to use with a father I didn't know.

He confessed he didn't remember much about his marriage or about us, really, though he'd tried his best when we were young. He spoke of how the early years shape you for the future, and seemed pleased that we were doing well in our lives. I wanted to shout *But it has nothing to do with you! You left when it mattered the most.* But I didn't say it, didn't yet know that I could give a voice to the little girl who'd been left behind. He admitted his marriage to our mother had been wrecked by his philandering and immaturity, but spoke warmly about his other children. It was obvious he'd mellowed, taking his role as their father far more to heart than he'd been able to do with us. He said he never let them go to bed unhappy. "I tell them not to worry about what happened in the day and that I love them. And then I give them a hug and tuck them in." I caught myself thinking what a nice dad this stranger sitting before me was— and then remembered that he was my father too, finally arrived seventeen years too late. I saw similarities between us. They were imperceptible at first, but as the afternoon wore on I saw myself reflected back in his mannerisms and sense of humor. I remembered how he'd had a certain charm about him, though I'd always put it down to a young girl's memory of her father rather than actual fact.

By the end of the afternoon, after such seemingly honest discussion, our small talk started to dwindle. We'd skirted around the possibility of meeting again and parted with hugs and tears on all sides. As we left, my sister said in bewilderment, "But I liked him," —we honestly hadn't been prepared for that. I cried going home, and the pain over the next few days was akin to that you feel at the end of a relationship, which, in a sense, it was. I had to relinquish some of my longstanding beliefs about my father; I had to try to find a place for the idea that he was potentially a nice person, someone I had even warmed to.

Alas, this story does not have a happy ending. One afternoon was not enough to heal the damage done. We spoke on the phone several times before he returned to Australia and exchanged a few e-mails in the months afterwards, but they inevitably dropped away. The last time I saw him, at my grandmother's funeral, was awkward and strange. He was there but he wasn't—nothing solid had been built between us, and there was much confusion and bad feeling floating around. It wasn't until I found myself in therapy years later that I understood how deeply embedded the wounds really were.

Bereavement broke me open, and sitting at the heart of the pain I found the little girl I once was, waiting to be acknowledged. This book you hold in your hands has been written for and by that girl too, and for all the younger selves we carry inside, who look to us for protection and love. We are their big sisters and brothers, their mothers and fathers. It has taken time to accept that this damaged little girl is still a part of me, the vulnerable, expectant, sometimes demanding part of myself. I grew up wary of men and to this day I do not understand the bond a father can have with his daughter; it will always seem strange and threaten me somehow.

When an interrupted childhood forces you to grow up too fast you're never in a hurry to revisit the past, so my younger self was abandoned twice—first by her father and then by me. But these younger selves wait quietly inside us until an opportunity arrives for their voices to be heard—a death, a divorce, a layoff, an accident; something big enough, and life-changing enough, to take our attention away from the everyday chatter, and focus on what matters most: our survival. It is into this space that the stories will be recited, louder and louder until you can no longer avoid them. A hurt experienced in the present opens the door to all the other hurts waiting in line to be felt and healed, and standing at the back of the line is a child, the very first incarnation of you.

Healing the past helps to heal the present. And like anything worth doing, the execution is considerably harder, but
not impossible. If we can find the courage to let that original
pain breathe we can burn through the discomfort and memories, we can get back to the origin of the story that hurts us,
and begin to let it go with love, with forgiveness, or whatever
else the phantom pain needs. It may take a weekend; it could
take years. We may carry the bruise till the end of our days,
but while memories cannot be changed, the way we view them
can. That is the one part of the story we control.

For a long time I thought I had to forgive my father for
leaving us, but I discovered I only needed to learn to love
the girl he left behind, something I resisted. "Why should
I try when it's easier to ignore her? I'm not that stupid girl
anymore." I was sitting across from my therapist when the
tears finally began to flow. "She was so needy and desperate. She clung to any man that gave her attention. How could
anyone love something so pathetic?" The tears continued,
along with the anger, as if by finally voicing the disgust I
ripped open a pocket of emotion held shut for too long. But
when I stopped the ranting, when the spiteful words abated,
I was left with a softness in the center of my chest and felt
the sadness of an eleven-year-old girl who'd been left
behind.

As the months passed I learned it was safe to connect with this younger part of myself. Just opening to the idea that she needed my compassion rather than my scorn brought profound healing; it had never occurred to me to be *kind* to her. As I grieved the loss of my partner I unraveled the binds from the past too, and the girl who'd read in bed by flashlight came out and showed me what she needed: some quiet time alone, hours spent dawdling in galleries, aimless walks along the beach. As I ventured back out into the world I took my younger self with me.

In time I realized the part of me I'd thought so needy was the part that nurtured empathy for others, that could hold another's heart without crushing it. Her softness was not weakness, as I'd feared: It was her gift. When I stopped and listened to what she was trying to tell me life seemed to flow so much more smoothly. By taking the time to explore this place inside me, healing the hurts and honoring the lessons, I remembered that it's okay to feel unsure—I don't always have to be the *brave girl*. My vulnerability is my strength, just as my apparent strength can sometimes be my vulnerability.

It's our responsibility as adults to look after children, and I believe this also applies to the children inside us. Your inner child may not be as messed up as mine, but I think most of us experience some sadness attached to our childhood—the mixed messages, confusion, expectations, and disappointments;

the crushes and hormones, the crippling peer pressure. Like matryoshka dolls, the children we once were live beneath the layers of selves we become over the years. It doesn't matter what age we are now—the influence of the past can often be felt as keenly as if it'd happened yesterday, so the more compassion I am able to show my younger self, the more healing I draw to other areas of the past.

It's a work in progress, as always.

reflection

I sometimes wonder about the true nature of time and space. I often feel like a multi-*generational* being, that inside this one body exists not only my younger self and the self I am now, but also my future selves, not least of which is the wise old crone I like to imagine I'll eventually become. I see her with long white hair and a wild look in her eye, a turquoise scarf knotted loosely around her neck. How wonderful it would be to have these multiple selves in a room together; I've taken to writing to them, to keep the conversation going. It's amazing what we know when we are given a voice.

Set aside an hour or so to write a letter to your childhood self. What do you want to tell her? What wise words do you have to share with your younger self, and how can you reassure her? Is there something she needs to hear? Maybe you want to tell her stories or impart words of encouragement—whatever comes to mind. Start with "Dear [your name] . . ."

Now imagine you're in your twilight years, in a comfy chair with a dog sleeping at your feet and a writing pad in your lap. The afternoon light is falling through the window, and you're warm and safe. Write a letter to yourself at your current age. With all those years and experiences behind her, allow your older wiser self to share the things she has learned about life.

What really matters? What stories did she let go of? Spend at least half an hour writing this letter from the future.

When you're done, put each letter in an envelope and mail them to yourself. You might like to include some other small gifts—a small bar of chocolate, perhaps, or a paper flower. A leaf from your garden. A special seashell.

When the letters come back to you, find some quiet time to read them slowly. First open the letter to your younger self and let her read what she needs to hear. You could make a favorite snack of years gone by; a glass of milk? A cheese sandwich? Whatever she needs, give it to her. Let her know how special she is. How special you are.

Next savor the wisdom of your future self. Read the words out loud to connect even deeper to what she has to share. Carry her words with you throughout the rest of your day.

When you have finished reading both letters tuck them into your journal or a bedside drawer. You can draw on the wisdom of your future self whenever you feel you need her wise counsel—all you have to do is pick up a pen and ask.

There is a lifetime of wisdom within you.

writing with my eyes

"We do not make photographs with our cameras. We make them with our minds, with our hearts, with our ideas."

—Arnold Newman

letting ourselves be seen is terrifying. I'm always in awe of people who can get up on stage and sing without embarrassment. I do not possess the gene that chases after the limelight—I can't think of anything worse. I prefer to be the one behind the curtain, tapping away at my keys, walking through town with my camera, recording the ordinary magic I see. When I have to put my work—*myself*—out there, I do it with as little fanfare as possible. Because that's when I feel the most vulnerable, when I'm sharing with other people, sharing my thoughts, my ideas, my feelings. It doesn't matter if it is done with paintbrushes, pianos, or Polaroids, if we put our heart into it, it will make us feel more exposed than just about anything else. We fear we'll look stupid, that we're opening ourselves up to ridicule, that we'll fall over in the playground and be laughed at. But the kid who laughs the hardest is the one inside our own head, the bully who pushes you back over as you're trying to get up. No wonder it's so hard to get paint on canvas or words on the page when we're judging the work before it even exists.

If your creativity is your bread and butter, then promotion is never far from your mind. If we're to have any hope of paying the bills each month we must learn to get comfortable sharing our vision with the world. The Internet has made it possible for creative people to share their work with a bigger audience than ever before. Publishing new work online—and getting immediate feedback—has become the norm. However, this new visibility can come with a sting in its tail. I was enjoying a procrastinatory meander through the blogosphere, hopping from link to link till I landed on a website I hadn't visited before. I noticed the artist was offering an online class, so I clicked over to read more only to be faced with the exact words from my own site, republished on her class page. It's heartbreaking to be stolen from in this way—and it did feel like theft to me, the words I'd spent hours honing taken with the click of a mouse. My immediate reaction was anger, followed closely by a sense of extreme violation—how dare she! With clammy hands I wrote a polite but firm e-mail to the artist, pointing out the theft and asking that she rewrite her page, ending with the ominous "I hope I will not need to take this matter any further."

Within ten minutes I had a reply, her profuse apologies spilling out on my screen. Half an hour later her page was rewritten. So I replied, accepting her apology, knowing it hadn't been her intention to hurt me. "The irony is," I told her, "now that you've made the changes I actually get a sense of what your course is about, in your own words, rather than a cut-out version of mine. Now I see what you are offering your potential students, and they will too."

"You are right," she replied, "I should have had more faith in myself all along."

And though I was still irritated, I did feel for her. Despite having devised a course out of her own ideas and passions, she hadn't trusted that her voice could sell it to others, so she used mine instead. It takes time to trust that our voice will be heard and to believe that we have something to say that's worth saying.

Words and images have always been the currency of my creative life, but it was years before I could stand up and say, *Yes, I am a writer, yes, I am a photographer,* as if I had to achieve a certain level of success before I earned the right to call myself either. When I say I am a writer I mean I use words to convey the truth in my heart. When I say I am a photographer I mean I use cameras to record and interpret the world around me. Of my two passions it's my photography skills I feel most confident about. For as long as I can remember I have "seen" photos wherever I go, noticing small details, colors, the lines and shapes that marry so well in a flat image. I notice how branches scratch across a blue sky; how the space *between* the cushions looks so soft and safe. There's a list in my head of my must-take shots, and I can't walk past a construction site without snapping the side of a rusty truck, a constellation of colors found in deceptively mundane places.

My eyes don't judge what they see—there's no hierarchy of beauty when everything piques your interest. For a time I thought that being a real photographer meant I needed to join associations and offer my hourly services to paying clients. So I tried it for a year, making postcards and advertisements, networking with the mothers at local schools, photographing christenings and birthday parties and families on the beach. And there were moments of real fulfillment—when clients loved their portraits and called to thank me, when I felt I'd captured something truthful in a family group—but the work drained me more than any job I've ever had, my introverted self exhausted by having to be "on" all the time. I'd turned my passion into a job, trying to fit into a mold that wasn't designed for me. So I spent less and less time on the marketing, until the phone stopped ringing and I recycled the postcards. Although it felt like a failure, I couldn't ignore the relief.

Photography is more accessible than perhaps it's ever been, with camera phones and social media feeding an unending stream of images into the ether. While potentially we're all photographers now, in truth it's never as simple as owning a camera. For me, a photographer is a person who expresses themselves using the photographic medium. They don't have to sell their images, or have clients or commissions—they are simply compelled to translate what they see and feel into a photograph. Most forms of creative expression require specific tools, but if you were to take away the paintbrushes and the cameras, the loom, the guitar and the stage, you'd be left with a bunch of people who are compelled to act on their creative impulses. You are left with *artists.* I believe we are all artists at our core, all of us endlessly creative, using our lives as canvases, our imaginations as tools. Children are born artists, seeing the potential in every cardboard box and dried leaf, remaking their world as fast as they discover it. We don't lose that innate creativity, but many of us repress it, weighed down by all the grown-up responsibility adulthood brings. But with a camera, a pencil, a ball of yarn, we can make something out of nothing; dinner served with a flourish, a bed made with vintage linens, a garden border planted with tulips. We simply need to open our eyes and put some thought into the details. We are the curators of our lives—we decide what they look like.

When I was a little girl I wanted to be either a vet or an artist; to my mind it was going to be cats, dogs, and bunnies, or stand-ing at an easel painting landscapes. I grew out of the vet idea

but couldn't shake the other. Art school was fabulously self-indulgent, cheap rent and student loans fueling three years of experimentation and practice. With a camera in my hands I had the missing link between my head and the world around me. I found my voice as a fledgling artist in a darkroom, poring over the contact sheet from the very first roll of film I developed myself. There'd been hundreds of snaps over the years but this was the first time I'd used a camera to *say* something. I shot my friends posing in various states of undress, my clichéd portrayal of female empowerment and strength. I shot nudes, fashion, street photography, and constant self-portraiture, all documenting the life of a nineteen-year-old girl. One image I remember from that time was a black-and-white studio shot I took of a friend; her head, arms, and torso bound with bandages, with just her eyes and one breast revealed. "What does it mean?" my instructor asked with a sigh, not the first time he'd seen such a shot, I'm sure.

"Does it have to mean anything?"

"All photographs mean something," he said. And of course it meant something to me, but back then I lacked the courage to articulate my feelings out loud. I wish I could go back in time and sit with the girl I once was. I'd tell her befriending herself is the way to find that love she craves, but I know she wouldn't hear me. There are parts of the past that we have to experience, chutes and ladders that take us across the board and get us where we're going. I wasn't ready for my world to unravel then; I had to get to London first and take a few more rides on the abandonment train before I was finally ready to heal my self.

Twenty years later and I still prefer to stay comfortably covered behind the lens, telling my story in more subtle ways. All the pieces fall into alignment when I see an image I want to capture—and it is a capturing, for the moment can pass as quickly as it was found. First I slow down. I see color and lines and shape and then, when the image falls together into a composition that pleases my eye, I hold my breath and press the shutter. The picture becomes a part of me because it was my eye that saw it; I create an impression of my experience on film, and everything felt in that moment is written across the image. I write with my eyes.

As artists our voice is the most precious thing we possess, a way of seeing the world that's unique to us and only us. Which is why it's so galling when others choose to take it as their own. I don't want my photographs to look like they were shot by Diane Arbus or Uta Barth—I want them to look like they were taken by me. While I'd never presume to have work that's even comparable to the photographers I admire, the work of those who've gone before me is embedded somewhere in my subconscious, feeding my visual vocabulary with imagery I conjure when composing a shot. Just as the writer learns how to write by reading, the fledgling photographer learns how to shoot by looking, first through her viewfinder and then through the eyes of others. This is a fertile time; the rules of composition can be studied and absorbed, but it is practice that creates the most improvement, returning to a shot, a scene, a place again and again, refining what you choose to reveal in imagery and emotion. I find myself increasingly drawn to simplicity, cutting away the extraneous words and possessions; my home becomes clearer, my language more concise. This is apparent in my photography too—for every chaotic shot there are ten that calm the eye.

I left art school not knowing how I could earn a living taking photographs. It was 1995 and I had neither the contacts nor the confidence to launch myself as a fine art photographer. So I carried on shooting for myself, and endured a series of unfulfilling jobs until I decided to go back to school to get a journalism degree. And while my years as a journalist looked good on paper, it wasn't work that lit me up—I had no idea what would, until life took me down a different path. In the depths of my grief I found my way back to the camera. Photography anchored me back into the world. Photography made me brave again, brave enough to take a stranger's

Sometimes
I'm a writer
who writes
with a camera;

sometimes I'm a
photographer who
shoots with words.

portrait in the street. Photography made me get on a plane to a place I'd never been before. I remember walking through Seattle's Pike Place Market, heading toward Starbucks—naturally—to wait for the rain to stop. I had a borrowed camera and the memory card was full so I was pointing out shots to my friends. Suddenly everywhere I looked there was yet another to be taken, the newness of the market, the city, the country washing over me like a sunrise. Raspberries falling out of blue paper cartons, purple lights reflected in the wet cobbled alleyway, an old guy playing guitar outside the coffee shop—I wanted to be taking the pictures. I should have been more prepared. I'd never used a digital camera before and didn't know that the memory card would fill so quickly. That night I deleted the photos I didn't like, ready to take more the next day. A week later and I was back home, looking through my images, getting more and more excited as I pieced them together, fashioning stories and vignettes out of my memories. That was the moment I became a photographer again, completing the circle from all those years ago. I'd created more than vacation snapshots—within each image was a piece of my healing, every detail I noticed was evidence my eyes were opening up, my soul connecting with something outside of me, the inward nature of my grief airing out, the light flowing back into my world.

When you're floundering in grief, photography can get you out of the house, while writing is a key for a different door. I find I do my most coherent writing at home, and create my best photographs when I'm outside. Photography feels like outward movement, reaching out into the world, my eyes open, creating new images. Writing, on the other hand, is an inward retreat, as I sink into myself to find the words, dropping into my body and swimming with the currents of my past, locating memories that hold clues to today. I'm easily distracted by social media and my phone, the kettle's constant rumbling, the siren call of the fridge. I need to feel safe to write, yet I feel so very bold when I shoot. Writing leaves me open, exposed, like I'm flashing my underwear. I write a lot of stupid things. I have a lot of stupid thoughts. Some days I think I don't know much at all, and yet I'm so compelled to share, knowing that in the sharing we find common ground, that my story might sing to your heart, just as your story calls to mine. The world is smaller when we tell the truth about our lives; how many times have I wanted to drop to my knees with gratitude when I found another soul who'd faced the fire of grief and survived? And with every e-mail I receive thanking me for my honesty, I remember that telling the truth about our lives is the best contribution we can make.

Sometimes I'm a writer who writes with a camera; sometimes I'm a photographer who shoots with words. There's no way I can show you my heart without including the Polaroids, just as the photographs are lonely without the words beside them. When I read I see images; when I take photographs I hear descriptions. This is my creative world, the two disciplines informing and supporting each other, my photographs telling stories, my words filled with images, the visual and the narrative fusing together.

As a child I'd cut up magazines and make collages in my diaries, fastidiously recording my days alongside pictures of the dresses I wanted to wear and rooms I wanted to inhabit. When my whole world broke apart on a Thursday morning my diary was there again. *"It's been eleven days since he died,"* I wrote, *"and still I don't believe it. I can even write the words down, but it cannot be true."* His death cleared everything away like a bush fire. I wrote for hours every day, a year-long love letter saying everything we'd left unsaid, hoping I could write my way out of the grief. And when I dried up and had no voice left, poetry pulled me back into my words.

Poetry is the scent of your lover's skin; it's standing by the ocean during a thunderstorm. It's the morning after a dark night of the soul, when the sun comes up and you make that first cup of coffee, knowing you've survived, knowing you're stronger than ever. Sometimes I reach the end of a poem wanting to tear the page out and eat it, to keep the words inside me—when you discover a poet whose words translate your experience of the world, you will be loyal to them forever. Erica Jong, David Whyte, Li-Young Lee, and Carol Ann Duffy were the wise elders I turned to in the quieter moments of my grieving, when the ruminating had ceased and I needed to taste more than ashes in my mouth. And then there was Sharon Olds, the high priestess of them all, her poems splints for my broken bones. There were days when all that entered my body was blood-red wine and her words.

When Olds came to England my friend Megg and I went to hear her read in a church in the middle of Bath. With the sun setting through the stained glass windows, she walked up to the microphone and sparkled, the light catching the sequins on her yellow and black skirt, the rhinestones on her glasses glittering, a diamante clip restraining her hair. Her hands shook as she began to read from a book of her own poetry, the audience absorbing each word like a congregation awed by a sermon. Her poems were personal and passionate, deliciously laced with humor in places—she knew how to work the crowd. I was so caught up in her world I forgot to note down the titles.

"As human beings we have a need to write poems," she told us in the interview afterwards. She said she writes her poems and diary entries in simple drugstore notebooks; that she writes longhand and fast, crossing out words as she goes, preferring not to use placeholders while she searches for the right word. She described the shape of her poems with her hands in the air, and told us she draws pictures in her letters, that her pen "wants to do different things." She was charming and earnest, admitting that she used her long silver hair as a shawl to hide behind in situations like these, which made the audience chuckle; I noticed a loose thread hanging from the hem of her sparkling skirt, catching against her black hiking boots.

After the talk came the obligatory book signing, the line snaking out toward the back of the church; I'd never realized there were so many poetry lovers in my city. It's such an intimidating experience meeting a person you admire. I had ninety seconds of her time while she signed my book, and after spelling out my name for her I quipped she could call me anything, that I really didn't mind. "But I like to use the right words," she said. And I felt so silly—of course she does! I wanted to tell her that her poems had helped bring me back to life, that she'd given me words when I'd had none of my own. I wanted to tell her that her words had become a part of me too . . . but I just said, "Thank you so much" and walked away, a little bit embarrassed and a lot in awe.

It's a blessing to find writers whose words speak for us when we are mute, the scribes who record our collective experiences and mine their own lives so we can better understand ours. If your calling as an artist is to write, it's a vocation that pays out twice: first to you as the detective unraveling your heart and then again to the reader who consumes your work. We don't write to be published—though publication may come—we write to make sense of the noise in our heads. We write to record memories and share what we know. We write to feel less alone, to confide our fears to the page. Imagine a world without love letters, without birthday cards and dedications. Our truthfulness can change a life—if not someone else's then at least our own. In a world swirling with thousands of languages, there is space for everybody to tell their story. Photographs, paintings, and music carry the essence of our hearts, but it's the words that tell the secrets.

Pick up a pen and claim your words. Leave messages to yourself in the sand and carve your initials on a tree. Write on the walls or on the back of a receipt: Just get it down.

Your words are powerful. Use them.

reflection

Over the years photography has become a form of meditation for me, a way to plant myself squarely in the moment and become more *present*. It doesn't matter if I'm in a new country or walking along my own street, with a camera in my hands I stop and record the scenes and things that catch my eye. I slow down and investigate; I climb on chairs and kneel in the dirt to get the shot. As I focus the camera I find my own focus too. One of my favorite photography quotes is something Dorothea Lange said: "The camera is an instrument that teaches people to see without a camera." The camera gives us a reason to *look*.

Pick one day this week to document in photographs, starting from when you wake up (remembering to put your camera beside your bed the night before) through to early evening. Aim to take a couple of shots every hour for 12 hours.

As you snap your way through the day try to let go of any expectations and *shoulds*—this isn't about doing something clever with your pictures; rather, use your camera as a documentation tool. Pay attention to the smaller moments you'd usually overlook—buying a parking ticket, locking the front door, standing in an elevator—what do you see? Bring your attention to the moments that aren't usually considered "beautiful."

Remember that this particular day will never happen again, so what makes it unique? A thought or feeling, a phone call, something you hear, something you remember. Record the golden yellow of your scrambled eggs, and the heart-shaped crack in the sidewalk.

Look out for moments you wish to cherish. When you collect your child from school, where do you stand as you wait for them? When making dinner for yourself, do you use a special glass for your wine? Or a favorite mug for your morning coffee?

Use the macro setting on your camera to record the details as if you were observing your day through a magnifying glass. Look for the texture of the fence you walk past every day or the gravel where you park your car. What does your bedroom floor really look like?

As you look back through your images of the day, what surprises do you discover? Try completing this exercise every month on both fun days out and the more regular days. Use your camera to slow down for a few moments.

Investigate your world as if for the very first time.

i have a body

"It's never been true, not anywhere at any time, that the value of a soul, of a human spirit, is dependent on a number on a scale."

—GENEEN ROTH, FROM WOMEN, FOOD AND GOD

Sometimes it seems I'm dragging my body through life, that it's a mass of flesh that weighs me down when my true self, my spirit self, wishes to fly free. I often have flying dreams, where I'm cruising along several feet off the ground, not swooping or diving, but a more realistic coast through the air while those all around me are trudging along on foot. Every time I wake from the dream I think it's real, that I *can* fly, I just haven't remembered how to yet. But how will we ever learn to fly when our bodies weigh us down so?

I step into this chapter cautiously, knowing I'm approaching the landmines that every woman deals with daily. Or maybe that's a sweeping generalization. Maybe there are women out there who do not think of their bodies in any way other than with complete acceptance and love, but I have yet to meet a woman like that. Instead, I know friends, students, acquaintances, and blog readers who struggle to see their own physical beauty, whose day-to-day experiences of themselves are littered with disappointment, frustration, guilt, and shame.

This is my daily experience too. My contentment has never been dependent on my dress size and I'm happy to buy clothes that fit properly and flatter my shape, no matter what number's written on the tag. But lately it's getting harder to ignore the way my body is changing. This body I have does not feel like me anymore—there are parts that are new, fleshy protuberances that rub and jiggle when I walk, pockets of fat that lurk accusingly under my skin. Every time I pull on my jeans I wonder if I'll be able to close the zipper, my loose pair now the tight pair that's left in the drawer. Walking up flights of stairs makes me sweat and pant, and hot summer days teach me why talcum powder is not just for babies. I never knew any of this before. I was the annoying girl with the "fast metabolism" who ate what she wanted, when she wanted. Food and I have always had an easygoing relationship. I've made my own yogurt and sprouted my share of beans; I was vegetarian for a few years and tried a zebra steak in Kenya. I like all vegetables except parsnips and can happily prepare the same dinner five nights in a row. I like food that seduces my taste buds and have always let that guide my meal choices. Sometimes food is just fuel that's shoveled into my mouth when I'm rushing to an appointment; other times, I know the chocolate I'm enjoying on the sofa is easing the lonelies that surfaced that evening. Once in a while I think there are foods I *should* eat, and suddenly preparing meals becomes a military operation: planning ahead and buying only the freshest ingredients, juicing and blending and soaking and measuring. It becomes yet another job, another set of rules, and even though I know this may be really good for me, my taste buds are craving doughnuts. I've never really been able to discipline my body; she does what she wants and I let her.

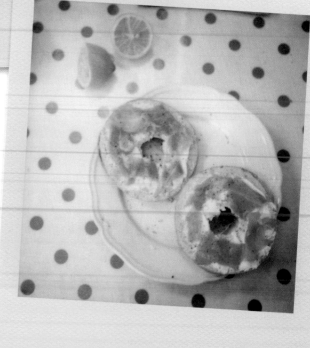

Choosing food because it tastes good makes sense when we're foraging in the forest, but in the twenty-first century I know my renegade taste buds are to blame for my wobbly bits. I like food and I like eating. I drank vineyards of wine and I smoked for twenty years because I *liked* it. But as I indulge in neither of these habits anymore, my food consumption has reached prodigious new heights. Some days my body feels like a science experiment; there's always something new to see and learn. And so here we are, my body and me, pitted against each other in a daily battle between what I want to eat and what I should eat, what I want to do and what I should do, what I want to wear and what I can fit into. I do not expect to be the size I was ten years ago; I know that just as my self takes up more space in the world, so too does my body. And I want to embrace that big-ness, the more-of-me-to-love-ness, but I can't deny the disappointment wrapped around my curves.

One of my earliest body memories dates back to when I was eight or nine: We'd returned home from a shopping trip, and my sister and I still had energy bubbling under our skin. We started jumping around the living room, lifting our hems up around our little tummies and twirling in circles, our delighted squawks echoing off the walls. Our glee only lasted a few minutes before my grandmother walked in and sharply told us to *pull our dresses down and stop showing off.* I remember feeling chastened and deflated, something I often felt around her, although I know she loved us. It'd be so easy to read more into this memory than is necessarily there, but it fascinates me that this is one of my key recollections from that time.

When I think of my body today, when I lower my awareness down into my bones and listen to the blood whizzing through my veins, I am still twenty-one. It is as if the benchmark for my physical self was set back then, forever my reference point when I stand in front of a mirror: How far away from that body am I today? With every year the distance grows, time measured in layers of fat around my middle like the rings of a tree. How can we love our bodies when they are under constant attack— from our expectations, from our judgments, from society, from others? No one can hurt me more than I can hurt myself, but I still remember past proofs of my imperfection: being told I had "sturdy calves" at school; a boyfriend admitting he wouldn't find me attractive if I put on more weight; telling a date I felt self-conscious about my stomach and hearing him say, "I see what you mean" as we canoodled at the end of the evening (he was not invited to stay the night). These little slights have stuck in my mind, times when I felt vulnerable and received confirmation of my fears, comments that weren't intended to hurt but cut away at my fragile sense of self nevertheless. Because the body is more than flesh and blood: It's our currency in a world obsessed

with sex and beauty, and no matter how much we fight it, we look at a stranger's face first to see if we recognize them and then to determine their attractiveness. Is he attractive enough to father my child? Is she more attractive than me—could she steal my lover? Even the birds primp and preen to attract the right mate.

I don't want my body to be all that's visible of me. It should be just one facet, the physical aspect that carries me around, but not so important that it disguises what else I am—my thoughts, my memories, my heart. I am so much more than the size of my breasts or the thickness of my eyelashes! If I must be judged let it be for who I am, not the firmness of my thighs. Still, as I sense my value as a sexually attractive woman lessening, there's a part of me who wants to be followed by wolf whistles as I walk down the street—I write that with a wry smile on my lips. Do shirtless men still hang like monkeys from scaffolding in this day and age? I'm guessing yes, just not in my vicinity anymore. It feels natural to want to be found desirable by men in this way, only a few evolutionary steps from being clubbed over the head and dragged back to a cave. My inner feminist may have shaken her fist at every unwanted flirtation, but boy, does she miss it now it's gone. These six years of self-imposed celibacy have healed my heart and cleared my mind, but I can't deny that I've missed the touch of another's hand, skin against skin, hard and soft entwined. He died at the height of our passion, when my body still ached for his. I learned to disconnect from the ache to protect myself, but how do I reconnect with my sensuality when I am on my own? Self-love takes many forms, and I've never been shy about my needs and urges. But making love is a gift you give to each other, and it's the cherishing that I miss today, remembering how it felt to be physically adored, my skin never softer, my curves never more luscious than when under his caress.

I do want my body to last an entire lifetime; I want it to run smoothly and painlessly, like a well-oiled lawnmower, the kind you drive around the yard, smiling as a mundane chore turns into an hour of fun. I want my relationship with my body to be *fun*, to be light and loving, a pleasure not an ordeal. I want to call a truce, to find a way to be a body *and* a soul, both at the same time. And just as I nurture my creativity and feed my mind with words and art, I want to learn how to nurture my body, to treasure the curves and the sags, and thank my feet every day for walking me to the supermarket without too much complaint. To remember to appreciate my arms that carry my groceries home, the finger that presses the shutter button, the knees that bend, the bottom that allows me to sit comfortably as I write these words. And my shoulders! How lucky I am to have them either side of my head, bearing the weight of the world as soundlessly as they do.

I want to learn to love my body again because it's the only one I've got.

⁓

Eight years ago I was lying naked on a beach in Portugal. Beside me was my friend, Carol, and a few feet away were Sarah and Leslie, lying on their fronts. None of us was wearing any swimwear. It had taken all of an hour for us to work up the courage to go commando, but after a bit of discussion, and a lot of laughter, we slipped out of our bikinis and lay back on our towels. I'd been topless on a foreign beach before, but this felt exactly as liberating as I'd imagined it would. We stayed on the beach for another hour before heading back to the villa, triumphant in our bravery.

By day two we were confident enough to try a dip in the ocean—bikini bottoms back on, naturally. We'd claimed a patch of beach hidden in the dunes and our group of four felt intimate, but not just because we were naked. I no longer noticed whether my bottom was larger or smaller than anyone else's—it just didn't seem important. On that second day we were sitting up and talking about life as we drew shapes in the sand with our fingertips. We ran back from the water's edge to eat sandwiches made from chunks of bread and ham, reclining on our towels,

languorous and giggly, not caring if our breasts drooped or bellies bloated. Suddenly skin was just skin, the sun kneading our flesh into the sand until all we could do was flop back and soak it in. I didn't feel vulnerable, and while there was a pleasurable sensuality to being naked outdoors, there was nothing sexual about it. It felt organic somehow, as if baring our skin to the elements simply made us a part of the landscape.

"I can see why nudists do it," Carol said, rubbing sunscreen onto her shoulders. "It's really freeing, like I don't have to pretend to be something I'm not—I'm just me, you know? I'm not hiding behind my clothes." She closed her eyes and let out a sigh. "I feel like I finally have some space." The breeze from the ocean was gentle, the sunlight clean and pure, making our skin more luminous somehow; I could see every hair on my arm as I brushed away the sand sticking to my thighs.

"But would you do it back home?"

Carol put the sunscreen back in her bag and reached for an apple. "No, it wouldn't be the same. It'd be too cold for a start." She laughed. "Besides, it's easier here—no one knows us."

For the rest of the week we drifted between the beach and the villa, cooking in sarongs, eating dinner by candlelight. Our nudity on the beach had broken down a barrier as we tumbled through the days alongside each other, not noticing the nakedness anymore as we sat on the veranda in bikini bottoms and smiles—I have the snaps to prove it. And I didn't see *naked* when I looked through the viewfinder, just women who were like me, women who liked food and also forgot to go to the gym. Each of us carried hurts from our lives back home, but that week on the Portuguese coast brought incredible peace, as we gave our heartaches over to the sunshine and salty water.

It saddens me to think that trip was the last time I truly felt connected to my body. In the in-between years there was a love that set me alight, his eyes, his touch accepting, loving every part of me, a gift I have never fully understood until now. I look in the mirror and wonder who could love me like that again. And that's when I hear it, the call to be my own lover, with my own appreciative eyes and touch, to see my body as whole and perfect exactly as it is. It was easy to bask in his gaze, to feel at ease in my skin because he adored me so, but it didn't come from within me. It was not of my own making. I mourned for his touch as much as I mourned for him, but all these years later it's my own acceptance I crave now. Relying on another to make us feel good only works as long as they are here; better to find it in yourself.

After the disembodiment that came with grief I've worked my way back into my skin, one sip, one mouthful, one inhalation at a time, creating a fuller expression of me, inside and out. And it's the *out* that caught up with me one morning as I walked home in the wintery sunlight from Victoria Park, feeling my thighs rub together, my breasts heavy, my shoulders ache. Out of breath as I walked up the hill and up the five flights of stairs to my front door, sweating, stripping my clothes off in the bathroom and running a shower, my body burning with the flames of exertion. I don't want to be constantly aware of my body, don't need to always know that I'm attached to the planet by gravity—heavy, ponderous, sluggish, slow. I hate that I tire quickly when I do anything physical, and that the majority of my wardrobe now pinches my flesh. I'm looking forty straight in the eye and suddenly, shockingly, I feel my age.

And this is where the discomfort comes from—this shock of aging. The realization that I'm entering midlife and there really isn't any turning back now. I can't rely on the invincibility of youth any longer, as I watch my body changing under the weight of all my years. And where I used to think I could just *get back in shape* whenever I wanted, I realize my body may have other plans. So if this is it, if this is the body I'm taking with me, perhaps it's time to get better acquainted with each other. Starting with the words I use to address it.

"You don't have a soul. You are a soul. You have a body."

I have come across this quote from C. S. Lewis countless times over the years, and every time I feel a jolt of recognition that, yes, I am not my body. I am more than that—I am a soul. This body carries me on the earth, but it is not who I am. But I wonder if that is truly the healthiest way to view this poor old sack of bones. Buddhists see the mind/body/spirit as inseparable. My friend Susan is a respected meditation teacher and lifelong student of Buddhism, so I asked her how Buddhists use the body/mind to feel more connected to something bigger than us. She wrote me straight back: "I think that the Buddhadharma would say that meditation is a way to *remind* us that the body/mind/whole/universe are already connected and that it is ego's 'job' to classify everything in separate boxes. But when we see clearly (as meditation trains us to do), we see that

there is only connection, only wholeness, only oneness. No separation."

She also told me that when Tibetan Buddhists say "mind," they point to their heart. This made me pause. I live so much of my life in my head, like a brain tethered to the earth by a body

I choose to ignore, yet through my healing I know my heart was where I felt my pain—literal aching at times, my grief made manifest within my body. And so it's all connected, but why is it so hard to remember this? What do I need to do to think of my body—my self—as beautiful again? To need nothing more than my own gaze to know that the curves and plateaus, the softness and dimples of the body that carries me is—that *I* am—beautiful.

As I lay in bed mulling all this over, I suddenly knew what I needed—before the gym membership, and the daily swims, and the time off to recharge. I need to forgive myself.

Forgiveness. What a lovely concept that is. It's a word that makes me think of flowing white robes and smiling benevolence; it's something I've had to cultivate in my life as a way to move through past hurts and let go of difficult feelings. But why is it so hard to forgive myself? I don't know where this expectation that I have to be perfect came from, but it's woven through my being like mold through stilton. Some forgiveness of my flaws, of my very human fears and frailties, would help me move forward with a kinder perspective; constantly beating myself up achieves nothing—I know, I've tried.

When we're blocked and can't seem to make headway with the things that are tripping us up, it's really just another opportunity to practice gentleness with ourselves, another chance to show ourselves kindness. Because contempt and disappointment really won't help. It's time to look honestly at the reasons for my changing size and to know that, when I'm ready, I can make different choices; I can work toward making changes; I can take each day as it comes, and if it's a day that needs a little extra sugar sprinkled on it then so be it.

When there's a lesson to be learned and I've trapped myself into a corner with my eyes shut and ears plugged, that's usually the moment a teacher appears in the shape of a trusted friend. Marianne arrived at my door carrying a small suitcase and a yoga mat, just like she did the first time she stayed at my house, during the in-between years when I was still unraveling so much of myself. I woke that first morning to find her practicing her *asanas* in my living room, while I, in contrast, brewed coffee and smoked a cigarette. Lithe and flexible, Marianne is a human rights officer who travels the world and changes it as she goes, her yoga practice a constant whether she's in Afghanistan, America, or a small Georgian flat in Bath with me. I admire her hugely and always feel changed after we've spent time together, her positivity and hopeful nature rubbing off on me in the best possible way. I made quinoa risotto and after dinner we drank a glass of red wine and discussed our book-writing progress. As we confided our fears and struggles, I suddenly blurted out:

"I feel like shit. I don't recognize myself anymore. I've been in such a good place emotionally, and am so grateful for all this work, but I'm so tired." My eyes filled with tears, always a sign that I've unlocked the truth. "All I want to do is lie down."

Marianne shifted her position to face me fully, one leg tucked under her. "When I've been working hard all week," she said, "I just want to crash at the weekend with a pile of DVDs, but I know it's not what my body wants. I've learned that my mind always wants to crash and relax, but my *body* wants to move. So I go for a run on the beach. It seems to help my mind too."

"I know my body wants to move—I can feel it. But I just don't have the time."

"This is a busy time for you, but even a few minutes of yoga in the morning will help. You could try ten minutes before you check your e-mail."

"But surely ten minutes isn't going to get me in shape?"

"Maybe not, but it's not always about getting fit, Sus— sometimes you need to look after yourself. To do something kind every day, even if it feels tiny."

The next morning we rolled our mats out on the floor and sat quietly. I felt a little shy and let Marianne guide me through a few poses. She taught me a fifteen-minute practice I could do on my own; it was simple enough for me, as the yoga-fearing novice, to understand, though I made copious notes just to be sure. Afterwards we lay quietly on our mats—eyes closed, palms facing up—and then hugged before I floated off to take a shower. I liked how calm I felt as I dressed for the day, starting the day in a quieter headspace. Since her visit I've practiced my morning routine off and on, diligently for the first few weeks, and then less so as I slipped back into old habits. Looking after ourselves requires such vigilance, such commitment, and it makes me realize I am not always as committed to me as I could be.

And there again is an opportunity to forgive myself. When I think of all the women I know who are battling these same feelings of disappointment and shame, who yearn to reconnect with themselves but lack the time or the energy or simply do not believe that they deserve it, I feel less alone in my struggles. I know I will never be a gym bunny who lives to "feel the burn," that my sybaritic tendencies will always have me reaching for an almond croissant and espresso over a sprouted bean salad, and I will enjoy *every single mouthful,* knowing in that precise moment my soul needs nourishment of a different kind. In many ways I want to take up more space in the world. After years of being lost, I'm working hard to be the fullest expression of me with friends and strangers, in my journal or in a grocery store: fleshy, messy, human me. There is room for all of us out there; we do not have to make ourselves small to fit into this world. We're together for such a short time, this body and I—when I remember this I let out a breath and sink into accepting that *this is all there is*. A body, a breath, a hunger for food, for love, for communion with others. This body is not all of me, but it reflects me so well. I let the world see my confidence when I straighten my back and walk tall; I reveal my late-night loneliness in the expanding curve of my hips. My body is a map of my life, a guidebook to my desires, and every day I add to the story. This chapter starts with a walk in the park and buying vegetables for soup tonight. Made with care and eaten with gratitude.

Will you join me?

reflection

We navigate the world through our senses. Sight, smell, hearing, and taste are received directly into our heads but touch is a full-body experience, unequivocally letting us know we exist. Right now I'm aware of the chair supporting the weight of my body; I feel the keys of the keyboard under my fingertips as I type. There's a bruise on my leg and when I reach down the mark feels tender to the touch. I pull a cardigan around my shoulders, the knitted cotton soft against the nape of my neck. This is where I am right now, sitting in this room, the touch of things around and against me confirming I am here.

Where are you right now?

What's touching your skin?

Take time to explore what it feels like to be inside your own skin as you move through your days this week. Put freshly laundered sheets on your bed and sleep nude tonight, reveling in the sensation of cotton against your skin. Brush your hair slowly, giving your full attention to every stroke, root to tip.

Is wool soft and cuddly or does it make your skin itch like mad? What are you wearing right now—can you feel it? Run your fingers across the fabric, search out the threads. Run your fingers down your arms . . . touch your left shoulder with your fingertips . . . touch your right knee.

If you're wearing shoes, take them off and feel the floor against your soles—can you feel the carpet? The wood? Place your feet squarely on the ground and stand up, feeling the weight of your body distributed through your feet, the backs of your calves, your knees, your hips. Relax your shoulders and take a few deep breaths—feel your lungs and ribs expand and contract.

Take a half hour walk with your camera and see how many different surfaces you can find and record. What does the outside of your house feel like? The bark of the tree across the street? When was the last time you touched the grass with your hands? Be a child again and for thirty minutes touch everything your eyes land upon, longer if you feel inspired. Use your camera to document every surface you encounter. If you prefer to write, take your journal with you and make lists describing the things you touch. Can you find ten different surfaces? Twenty? Let your hands be your eyes. Go barefoot outdoors and let your feet get muddy. Lie back on the grass (or the sand) and close your eyes, allowing the force of gravity to gently push you back against the earth.

Let your body become a part of the landscape.

look me in the eye and tell me you don't love me

"To support only one kind of beauty is to be somehow unobservant of nature. There cannot be only one kind of songbird, only one kind of pine tree, only one kind of wolf."

—CLARISSA PINKOLA ESTES,
FROM *WOMEN WHO RUN WITH THE WOLVES*

Out of all the women I have ever known, I can think of only one who truly relished having her photograph taken. Some were ambivalent, most actively hated it, but Corinne loved it and would suggest we take pictures whenever we got together. Her big dream was to be the star of a musical and she certainly had the personality for it: exuberant, bubbly, a bit of a show-off—in an endearing way, don't get me wrong. She was like a gymnast on the dance floor and loved being the center of attention—my opposite, in other words. Perhaps this was why, in images, she took on the role of my alter ego. Her confidence in front of the camera spilled into her life—she had insecurities like the rest of us, but when it came to her face, to her sense of herself as an attractive woman, she seemed solid. We lost touch when I moved away and I haven't seen her in years. I often wonder how she's doing and if she still buzzes around cameras, if her tremendous self-confidence has continued to grow or been eroded by the sobering effects of aging.

After he died I avoided the mirror, dressing quickly in the morning if I dressed at all, swaddling myself in comfortable layers. The days I applied lipstick to leave the house were noted as small achievements, but my appearance was of little concern to me back then, the mirror only reminding me he couldn't see me, and never would again. As therapy and medication pulled me back to myself I began putting more effort into my appearance, venturing out for a hair cut and painting my toenails once in a while. I felt less guilty spending time on me and pushed through the *What's the point?* negativity that jabbed at my side. A few weeks after the first anniversary I was clicking around on the Internet when I found a link to an online journal—my first ever blog discovery. The deeper I dug into its archives, the more links I found to other sites, until an entire creative community opened up as I jumped from blog to blog. I discovered spaces filled with photography and words and music and friendship; it was like finding a shelf lined with incredible books that never ended. I was hooked.

At first I lurked, peeking into the lives of women around the world and enjoying the thoughts they shared. But the day came when I read a post that spoke to me so directly, I had to leave a comment. The blog belonged to Denise, a photographer living in California, and to my surprise and delight she wrote back the next day, and we launched into a flurry of e-mailing. A year after he'd exited stage right, a new friend came into my world encouraging me to open up and let my new skin be seen. After a few weeks of mutual girl-crushing I wanted to send her an up-to-date photo of myself, right there and then, wearing the face I'd pieced back together. With a borrowed camera and a smudge of lipstick, I looked my reflection in the eye and pressed the button. The flash fired, so I switched it off and took a few more, but it was that first shot—the mistake, with a white light shining where my heart would be—that captured me best. I looked reserved but friendly, tired but alive. I thought I'd winced, but the woman in the photograph was smiling shyly, her face tainted with a knowing that was more likely tiredness. For once I didn't rip the image apart. I looked at my face, bigger than life-size on my computer screen, and I saw someone I recognized. That evening I sent the photo to Denise. "This is the first photo of me I've taken in a long time," I told her. "This is what I see in the mirror."

Looking at the photo now is like looking at the face of my own child. Thirteen months in and she's weathered the worst of the storm, finding her feet and shining a light out into the world, so that five years later it reaches my eyes, a blazing supernova. Yet as clearly as I see my heart written across that woman's face, how I wish it wasn't accompanied by a narration of comparison: *I looked so young back then!* It gets harder to look at photographs of myself with every year that passes, harder to ignore the gray hairs and lines that seem to deepen overnight; so many changes I can't control. I look into the mirror and see the memory of the girl I was, the hope of the girl I want to still be, and the shocking evidence of the woman I really am—surely that can't be me in there, with the softening

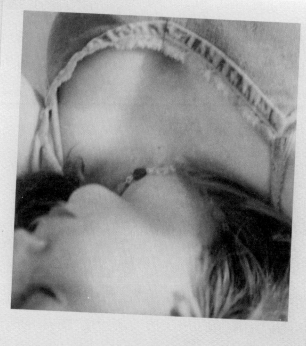

jawline and drooping eyelids? My complexion is fair and freckled, and the aging process is not flattering me. On the days I don't wear makeup I look hung over, and while there's a part of me that really doesn't care about all this, there is another that feels so cheated she wants to scream. I don't want any of this to matter, but it still trips me up when I'm tired and hormones are beating me down.

Whether in a mirror or a photograph, we regard ourselves through a pane of expectations, and when we don't see what we want to see, the *nots* rush in: not pretty enough, not young enough, not slim enough, *not good enough*. The need to be good enough stems from our need to be loved, the belief that love only comes when we're acceptable in the eyes of others. *If I'm pretty enough, he will notice me. If I'm slim enough, he will desire me.* We are not born with these thoughts—we learn them. We look for approval from our parents, our peers, and finally ourselves, the latter being the hardest prize to win. When I consider a lifetime of not feeling good enough, I know that it began after my father left, but there are so many more layers that I've absorbed since then. Was it the teenage years spent reading *Vogue* that messed me up? Perhaps it's too easy to blame the media reflecting the fantasies of a youth-obsessed culture back at us. Yet here I am, knowing better at the end of my thirties, and I still don't feel enough.

I stopped reading women's magazines a long time ago, tired of the teen models and digitally altered perfection; my years working as a fashion editor were enough to know that I did not belong in that world. I was an interloper sitting behind the coveted front row, women in front of me clutching handbags that cost more than my rent. The models appeared one by one, diaphanous dresses whipping at their heels; I tried to make notes on the colors and fabrics, but I didn't want to wear those dresses, and neither would my readers. *It's fantasy and commerce* said the powers that be, but the fantasy attacked the softest part of my being—beauty looks like this, it said, so this is what you must aspire to. The pecking order at the shows was terrifying, fashion students scratching at the door as the editorial contessas swanned out, their juniors following close behind. And then the models would reappear, rushing to their next show, all smoky eyes, skinny jeans, and sneakers. I lasted two years in that job, trying to do it my way, writing about clothing that flattered. Having to bow to the whims of my editor—No green clothes! She hated green!—gave me little room to maneuver. The day I handed in my notice was a nose-dive into a scary but welcome unknown. I never looked back.

Why is it so hard to think well of ourselves? To look at our own faces without judgment or criticism? Or worse—to ignore our reflection altogether. To rush though our days looking after everyone else, collapsing into a bottle of wine in the evening, not even noticing that another twenty-four hours have passed without a thought spared for our own selves. Too busy. Not enough time. Or maybe too scared to look. Lately my daily morning practice has been to try to look at the woman in the mirror with kind eyes. I brush my hair, noting the sleep creases on my cheek and the red-rimmed eyes—and I give that woman a small smile, raising an eyebrow as if to say *here we go again.* Most days that's all she gets; on exceptional days she may get a wink too because it makes me laugh at myself. I look at the woman in the mirror and do my best not to judge her appearance—it's not easy. The first glance always triggers the checklist that scrolls through my head: the state of my complexion, the deepening frown lines, the growing double chin, the yellowing teeth. That's when I catch myself and pull back my focus, taking in my head and shoulders, brushing my hair and trying for a smile. Standing there scowling at my reflection is not helpful. Besides, smiles are nature's face-lifts.

At first I felt ridiculous, self-conscious even, as I stood there alone. What kind of inane vanity was this to be staring into the mirror like a self-absorbed teen? But I persisted. Every morning it gets a little easier, and it never takes more than thirty seconds. Just a flash of a smile, an acknowledgment that I'm there—that I exist. Even on my down days, I try. I spent too many years shunning that woman, when all along she's been my most stalwart ally, waiting for the day I finally saw her: a woman who's doing her best; a woman who has made it this far, despite my best attempts to keep her down.

The recognition of this mirror self began around the same time I started blogging—therapy and writing were a dynamic combination. I'd seen other bloggers sharing self-portraits and felt emboldened to do the same. And while the photos I shared had a quiet strength, I wasn't ready to look directly into the lens. Still, the images were a significant milestone, not least of all because I posted them online. By revealing my face—the *outward* expression of who I am—I experienced another layer of healing. For so long there was only one person that I wanted to see me, one person who seemingly knew me inside and out—how could I let myself be seen if he could no longer see me? As I wrestled with this thought, a desire to see *myself* emerged, to become better acquainted with the woman I was becoming. Naturally my first reaction was to think that this is wicked vanity on my part. Who taught me not to show myself off? My Victorian

Photographing your own face is an empowering experience, but it will also throw up every negative thought you've ever entertained about yourself.

grandmother? Me? *Don't make a fuss, Susannah. Pull down your skirt, pull up your socks. Don't draw attention to yourself.* But despite the ghostly voices chiding me in my head, I still posted the pictures on my blog, my portal into the world at large. And though I worried I was revealing too much, when I sat with the question there was only one response: *You are claiming your space.*

Photographing your own face is an empowering experience, but it will also throw up every negative thought you've ever entertained about yourself. I've taken enough portraits over the years to know most women examine photos of themselves with incredible bias, looking for confirmation that their internal list of Not Good Enough is indubitable fact. It doesn't matter how anyone else responds to the picture, the subject rips it apart, dismissing image after image until, at last, we find the holy grail and she says what I've been waiting to hear:

"That one's not bad, I guess."

Miraculously a photograph has captured the way she wants to see herself, better composed images rejected in favor of the shots that make her look younger or slimmer or whatever it is she needs to see. With all the mean-lipped, snaggle-toothed photos of me littering the highway of my life, I understand completely. A flattering photo is a precious thing indeed—it's human nature to want our best selves portrayed, even if we may not be the best judge of what that really looks like. "Make me look nice," we beg the photographer. "Make me look *better.*" I spent my teenage years convinced that if I could just be photographed by a professional photographer all my ugliness would melt away, the real me would finally be captured on film (the "real me" looking uncannily like Christy Turlington). Now that I'm the photographer, I know that looking good on camera has very little to do with our attractiveness and everything to do with our bone structure and genes. Of course, the forensic clarity of a digital image does not help our cause, our perceived imperfections blown up to poster size on the screen, every freckle and stray hair wilting under intense scrutiny. Oh, to return to the days of Instamatics and blurred holiday pics. Perhaps that's why I fell so hard for the soft tones of Polaroid film. And while I relish capturing the world through my lens, it's others' responses to the Polaroid portraits that bring me the greatest joy. Today original Polaroid film is so scarce I only shoot three or four shots when taking a portrait, often making just a single precious exposure. Without the luxury of one hundred chances to get *the one,* the session becomes an exercise in

mindfulness; with only one shot I'm not looking for perfection—
I'm looking for the truth.

I'd been wanting to take Melissa's photo all weekend, and
on the last day of the art retreat in the woods of New Hampshire,
we left our pals to their farewell hugs and ventured outside into
the sunshine. The green wooden bench had witnessed many
portraits that weekend, and, gently brushing her hair back from
her face, I asked her to close her eyes. Immediately her features
relaxed as she let out a breath. I focused on her eyelashes and
then asked her to open her eyes and look at me. "You are so
lovely," I said as I looked through the viewfinder. Her shy smile
widened, her head tilting a little to the side; it was a playful
dance between us, as I leaned in closer, waiting for the right mix
of light and expression. I told her to think of John, the guy she'd
been sweetly flirting with the last few days . . . and there it was:
the softening of her face followed by a delicious twinkle in her
eye. I held my breath as I fired the shutter and pulled the photograph from the camera. The dance had taken less than a minute.

I sat down beside her on the bench as we waited for the
image to develop. The outline of her face appeared first, then
her hair, her smile. Her eyes were shining, the light catching
them *just so*. She gasped a little. "Oh wow!"

I held the photo to my chest to tease her. "It needs a couple
more minutes."

"Let me see!" She laughed and I placed the image into her open hands.

"This is how gorgeous you really are," I said, and I meant it. The camera and the film are simply the tools I use to capture what I see—what she might not see, or believe is there. I love to take portraits of women, to gift them with evidence of their beauty and spirit. When shooting friends the rapport between us helps put them at ease as I peer through the viewfinder. I usually have an idea of how I want to capture their face—maybe it's their smile I'm particularly drawn to, or a certain angle I've noticed as we talk. Helping them relax is essential, as is tuning in to how they're feeling—if I sense any embarrassment or discomfort I stop and we chat some more, until she knows she's safe with me. As Melissa and I said our good-byes I promised to send her a scan of the Polaroid. "Don't forget," she whispered in my ear as we hugged.

It was on the same trip that I shot my first Polaroid portrait of a man. I spent a few days in Cambridge, Massachusetts, getting over my jet lag before driving to the retreat, and had arranged to meet my new friend Chris for lunch. After two hours of nonstop talking it was time to say good-bye, so I asked if he minded me taking his portrait—like the true gent he is, he said he'd be honored. I got him to sit on a step so I was positioned slightly above him, then focused on his eyes, said

something silly to make him smile, and pressed the button. It took less than a minute. As the image emerged in my hand I was happy to see that it was correctly exposed with a soft flattering focus—and Chris was smiling. "You look great!" I said, showing him the Polaroid. "What do you think?"

"Well," he said, picking up his bag. "It's my face."

"But do you like it?" I asked, a little taken aback. "Does it look like how you see yourself?"

"It's fine," he said, looking bemused. "It's just a photo of my face."

Reader, this rocked my world so hard I thought my legs were going to buckle. *Just a photo of my face?* Where was the angst? The analysis? That was when I realized that men and women have very different attitudes toward how they look. I've been in relationships with men who spent their fair share of time in front of the mirror, so I know this isn't the truth for all men, but Chris's neutral reaction to his portrait—neither elation nor disappointment, just a measured acknowledgment of his own face—was a revelation. How freeing it must be to look at your own face without emotion, to see your eyes and nose and mouth and simply think, *yes, there I am.*

A week later I was standing in front of Rockefeller Center in New York City. It was my first visit, and judging by the number of people taking photographs around me I was not the only one. I'd pulled out my SX-70 to take a few shots of the scene when I was approached by a man in his early sixties. He introduced himself as Carl and complimented me on my camera; as he was sporting an old Leica M4 around his neck we immediately started talking about the joys of film photography. (A side note: Walk around any city in the world with a vintage camera in your hands and you'll be amazed by how many people stop to chat with you. It's the most wonderful conversation starter.) After an enjoyable ten minutes of friendly banter, I asked if I could take his portrait, and he smiled and said yes. As I'd done with Chris the week before, I shot a single Polaroid and showed it to Carl, asking what he thought. This time the reply wasn't so neutral: "Christ," he said. "I look just like my father."

No matter what age, sex, or nationality we are, we all look at our faces and see *something*. Carl saw his father looking back at him, Melissa saw evidence of her beauty, and Chris simply saw himself. Whether we like it or not our faces carry our histories, an ever-shifting map of who we are and where we've been. I took a lot of portraits on that trip, but it was the reactions of those three souls that reminded me what a privilege it is to be entrusted with someone's face.

⚬

I yearn to inhabit my skin with confidence and conviction.

I knew these words would need to be accompanied by a self-portrait or two, and I won't to lie to you: I'd rather not have my face printed on these pages. That a photographer hates having her picture taken is not so unusual; it's much safer behind the camera, watching the scene play out. Yet here I am, five years after e-mailing a photo to California, sharing my face in a book. You will note I've selected flattering shots, the softness of the Polaroid film smoothing out my skin, my features slightly out of focus, as I held the camera in front of me and took the shot. Just as it took me months to build up to sharing a self-portrait on my blog, I take a deep breath and know that these records of my face will be appreciated by my future self, the one with long white hair and a cat curled up on her lap.

So many of the difficult parts of our lives can be helped with a little kindness, and nowhere is that needed more than the way we view ourselves. If we cannot be kind to ourselves, how can we be kind to anyone else? It's easy to give love to my family and friends, but to then turn around and ridicule my own reflection so heartlessly surely takes the power out of the love I give. When I read about the cruelty and abuse that

happens every day in every corner of the globe, I wonder if it stems from a generation of lost souls who dislike themselves so intensely they take it out on others. And when I look in the mirror and see only the bad, the unworthy, the downright ugly, I abuse myself again and again, undermining the healing I've worked so hard to bring into my life. If by healing my grief and finding my way back to wholeness I honor the one I lost, then surely I dishonor him by thinking so little of the face he loved? We can use selective vision when we look at our reflections but the people we love see so much more—they see all of us: their sister or their friend, their mother or their wife. They see the stories we've shared and the places we've been together; they don't see crow's feet or double chins—that version belongs to us alone.

When I see someone I love I automatically smile at them—my face lights up, just as when they see me they smile too. It's human nature to feel and show pleasure when faced with an object or person we value. With that in mind, I will continue with my daily morning smiles, trusting that the day will come when I can look at a photograph of my face and say, *yes, there I am*, without conditions or labels—to simply see what's there: my eyes, my lips, my head attached to my body. I want to walk along the middle road, between vanity and not caring; I want to be seen and loved by the person I need it from most. To look in the mirror and smile at an ally I can always count on, the girl who overcame her fuckups and fears, the woman who has seen things she'll never forget. The lover who gave with all her heart; the griever who survived the depths of her pain. I want to cherish my imperfections as perfectly mine, and braid the hairs on my chin with ribbons and bells. My worth is not measured by my outward appearance, my worth is felt in my bones, in the quiet *yes* that starts in my belly and rises up to my lips as I reach forward and embrace my life, my world, this piece of experience that is mine alone.

I am an original. Unique. And every day I will do my best to remember this and graciously accept the extraordinary me-ness that is not ego or arrogance, but a gentle and humble recognition of the fact that

there is only one of me.

Just like there is only one of you.

reflection

I am thirty-eight years old, and I know that for some this sounds old and for others very young. We walk through this world with the past and future pulling us back and forth like bungee cords; the trick is to find the comfortable middle ground and inhabit our age with determination and grace. I look at photos of myself from ten years ago and wonder why I thought I was fat—I didn't know then that that was the best I was ever going to look. Now I look at myself and compare bumps and sags, forgetting that in ten years' time I'll look back and wonder what my problem was.

It's time to remember. It's time to see ourselves with kinder eyes and remember that the miles we've walked and the battles we've fought brought us to this point . . . right now.

This is who we are today.

Pick up your camera and take a photograph of yourself in whatever way feels most comfortable to you: it could be your feet, your face, your reflection. Take as many shots as you need to get one that you truly like. Take hundreds if necessary and remember to delete with abandon! Using either a professional lab or your home printer, make a hard copy of the photo so you can write a note to yourself on the back, jotting down a few words of encouragement, a short love letter, a gratitude list of the blessings in your life right now. For example:

Dear me, you always do your best, and your best is always enough. You are enough. I am so proud of you. All my love, me. x

If the words do not come easily try writing just three: I. Am. Unique. Let the words dance between your fingertips— there is only one of you in this entire cosmos. *Only one!*

Keep your love-letter-photo in your wallet or journal, or frame it and display it where you'll see it every day. Write a new love letter to yourself every month, taking more photos or investing in a professional photo shoot if your budget allows. Record who you are at this time in your life—

celebrate how far you have come.

CHAPTER 7

a tribe of one

"For now she need not think about anybody. She could be her-self, by herself. And that was what now she often felt the need of—to think; well, not even to think. To be silent; to be alone."
—VIRGINIA WOOLF, FROM *TO THE LIGHTHOUSE*

this morning I lit incense while the kettle rumbled, drawing back the curtains to wake up the living room. Sitting down on the sofa with a mug of coffee in my hands, I listened to the morning rhythm of the street: a car starting, a front door slamming, my neighbor's coughing fit. I sipped my coffee while coming down from my dreams—they take me so high the re-entry can be bumpy. Sometimes I dream he's still alive, but doesn't want to see me—his death was faked and nobody told me. Sometimes my dreams take me farther back to old loves; back to my mother's house; back to the good girl hiding in her bedroom upstairs, an invisible demon about to attack. It takes a while to shake them out of my head. Before I launch into my morning routine, before I even truly open my eyes, I try to get a sense of what the day will bring; I think of who I have to e-mail, what I have to write, what fires may need putting out. And then a tentative string of words starts to form, luring me back to the page, and with a dramatic shrug of the duvet, I'm on my feet, walking into the kitchen, coffee beans to find and grind. The morning ritual begins.

This is the quietest and most introspective time of my life, and I'm reveling in it, knowing only too well that one day the winds will change and I'll be facing another landscape. There may be children; there may be a man. There will definitely be new goals and challenges. But for now there's just me to worry about, and every day I thank my stars that I can sit with the sounds of the morning without mourning, that those days are behind me, my time filled with thoughts of today, this moment, right now. I sit quietly with myself, preparing for a day of writing, no longer gripping the past as an anchor, and trusting that the future is out there, somewhere. Some days I can't quite believe I made it to the other side, floating weightless in the sweet relief of silence.

The challenge of living alone and working from home is to not turn into a hermit, not an easy task when the quiet wraps around you so seductively. For me, solitude is not an empty space, but a richly detailed tapestry of my interests, thoughts, and desires. When I am alone I am free to dance inside the textures of my dreams without the pull to be elsewhere, the constant nagging feeling that I should be doing something else. In my solitude I am free to be me; I don't feel lonely for I am in my own company, and most days I cannot think of better company to be in. Being my own sidekick has its benefits—we like the same music and read the same books. But I also know that it's a luxury, the gift of all this time to myself. I try not to squander it, though the hours lost in the Internet black hole are legion. Solitude is a practice, and the more we experience, the easier it is to sink into the calm of uninterrupted time alone, amusing ourselves like children playing with buckets of mud. Do you remember the days when time stretched out like the long

For me, solitude is not an empty space, but a richly detailed tapestry of my interests, thoughts, and desires. When I am alone I am free to dance inside the textures of my dreams without the pull to be elsewhere, the constant nagging feeling that I should be doing something else.

shadows from the afternoon sun? When all we needed was a blanket and two chairs to enter our own magical kingdom?

A friend once admitted to me that she hated being alone, that when her son was with his father she'd arrange a full weekend of activities to stave off the loneliness. I watched her doing this over the years, her house always filled with friends and neighbors, Christmas parties arranged, the phone constantly ringing. Her life appeared full, but underneath I could see the past hurts she ran from. Back then I was locked inside my hermitage, venturing out once a week for coffee or groceries, but preferring to sink into the alone as my safe place to grieve. Yet I remembered that fear of the quiet, when thoughts were so loud the radio couldn't drown them out. We fear what we'll find in the alone. Boredom? Loneliness? Space for the guilt and shame to surface, the regrets and doubts we don't want to hear? We fear feeling friendless and abandoned by our loved ones, that we're exactly as unlovable as we believe ourselves to be. Better not to know, to fill our time with work and relationships and a bottle of wine with colleagues we don't even like. Years later and our life is ruled by domestic routines that we occasionally begrudge but carry out with love, and suddenly time for ourselves is craved but never found. We're spread so thin there's nothing left for us. But here's the thing:

Time alone is as essential
as breathing.

Time to check in with ourselves, to sit in the core of who we are and uncover what's really going on in there. If our cells are repaired while we sleep, then our heart is renewed in the quiet of the alone. And it's there in the stillness that we truly get to know ourselves, learning how to live with genuine curiosity and desire, rather than need and avoidance. I know there will be times when I fall flat on my face, but I stumble in my own shoes, no longer trying to be something I'm not. Finding a way to exist comfortably in the alone—sometimes busying yourself with projects and books, sometimes sitting still in the silence— is a step on the path toward self-acceptance, gently holding the fullness of ourselves the way we would a newborn baby.

I believe in the power of solitude to heal the heart, fac- ing up to our true selves without interference or intrusion. A period of solitude after any loss is critical for healing to take place, for how can we possibly identify the broken parts if we're numbing ourselves with alcohol, food, work? I did all this and more, and it worked for a time, but every hurt I'd encoun- tered along the path was waiting to be felt when my final crash came. We each experience bereavement in the way we need to, be it with company or alone, away from the blast or crouched in the ashes; the stages of grief are universally shared but the loss is as unique as the person who died. My grief demanded space, acres and acres of time on my own to sit with my new reality, measuring the absence of him. The first year was the transition from my old life into the new, the embarrassment of a Saturday night alone at home a hangover from my old city life, my new existence still undefined. At first the alone was excruciating, a continual punishment as ghosts and memories beat me down. But living so squarely in the pain I had no choice other than to relive my loss day after day until it became the foundation of a new life, one where he was not. Eighteen months in and that seemingly empty time was being filled with remade routines, my home a part of my new identity; four rooms to lay out my new self and discover I liked to arrange my bookshelves by color, not title. Little by little I befriended myself, learning how to live on my own as an individual, no longer defined by any other person. No one living, anyway.

We live in a world filled with constant noise, so when we withdraw to find a quiet nook for ourselves, the silence can seem so empty. My instinct is always to reach for a book or escape into a film, maybe dip into conversations on the Internet . . . but I stop myself. By leaning into this space we practice listening for the voice that's buried under our daily to-do lists; it's the quiet voice that's been waiting to be heard, the voice that speaks of our deepest truths. Sometimes I'm met with surfacing emotions I'd rather not feel, but instead of pushing them back down I try to ease into them, taking deep breaths and closing my eyes. My feelings tell me I'm alive, and even on my most deflated days, I know I mustn't avoid them, that they'll only return another time—better to push on through the sadness or sour-faced ennui I'm feeling that day. If this sounds overly conscious and methodical it's because sometimes it is, especially on the days I'd happily reach for the TV remote and slide into another world. But every so often I'm cradled in the feathery softness of silence and rather than reach for mindless distractions I open my journal and begin to write. I can fill my time alone with a hundred and one activities, but when I let myself slow down and tune into my own heart I find clarity, even if what I'm feeling is far from peaceful. The stillness of the morning and the quiet of the night are the times I feel furthest from being alone, when I'm in deep communion with myself, writing, reading, cooking dinner. After a lifetime of expecting others to make me feel better I've learned how to look after myself, in whatever way I need. I can cherish those quiet times, no longer fearing that they're all I have, knowing that they're exactly what I need right now. And when I do have company I'm so much more present with my friends, washing down our lunch with laughter and silliness, no longer keeping a foot out the door,

expecting to be someplace else. I listen harder and I love fiercer. Everything I need is right here with me

Even before grief taught me how to be alone, I had a keenly developed sense of my own personal space, wrapping myself in a cocoon wherever I happened to be. The day I realized I was an introvert was the day my life suddenly made sense to me. That needing time to decompress after I'd spent time with other people didn't mean I was antisocial—I simply draw my energy from the inside rather than the outside. I can party with the best of them, but my preference will always be to stay close to home.

The alone protected me while I healed, and now it's the space I use to conjure dreams from the ether. Would I have found my path if he was still here? I will never know the answer. Is it possible to sink into the alone while sharing your life with a mate? This question makes me pause. I fear the absence of time for myself as much as the absence of future love. I sense my next lesson being sent down the wires—how to retain this delicious wholeness while integrating another human being into my life. Because I know my selfish side will guard her space—after working so hard for it, I don't want to ever let it go. Yet I can't deny the other part of me that misses having a companion, who knows that Sunday mornings are even better with a warm body to snuggle next to. How to be alone while being together?

Historically, I have always lost myself in relationships. For the first three decades of my life I was out of balance. With no father to learn from, the masculine side of my being was chronically underdeveloped, the shy unconfident girl quickly developing into a sexually precocious teenager—there was no promiscuity, just an acute awareness of my feminine wiles and a desperate search for a *boyfriend*. I took dating extremely seriously, setting up home with my first love at seventeen, needing that sense of security, no matter how he felt about it. In retrospect, it's clear I was trying to correct the imbalance, albeit in my own dysfunctional way, but I didn't understand this at the time. My sole mission in life was to be part of a couple, the angry adolescent growing into a needy young woman. Two halves making a whole—but it didn't really work like that.

I once met a woman at a party whose words have always stuck with me: "Boyfriends come and go," she said, refilling my wine glass, "but my work is always there for me. It's this rock I have in my life I can always rely on." She was an artist living and working in London, her arresting portraits selling for thousands. At the time she was dating a much younger guy and I was at the tail-end of my ten-year relationship. Her world looked so much brighter than mine, her independence so alluring and healthy compared to my messed-up head. I still loved him, but it was a fraternal love, and the codependence that bound us together was suffocating us both. Every day had become an ordeal to be endured, the endless talks about whether we could fix things and whether we really wanted to. We both knew it was the end, we just hadn't found the guts to say it out loud. And then here was the artist living life by her own rules. As we talked that night I savored every word she said, imagining what it would be like to live so freely, committed to my work and dating guys for the hell of it, rather than as a Band-Aid for my broken psyche. And then my thoughts turned to the handsome man I had waiting in the wings, of how I ached to be close to him and feel his hand on my thigh. Because if your whole world revolves around another person, you'd better make damn sure there's another rock to jump to when you ditch the one you're with. And I did jump, just a few weeks later, and because I couldn't face being alone I fell into the arms of another man, my head a mess, my heart wide open. This passionate dance left me spinning—until the unthinkable happened and two years later he was dead. There was no more jumping then, nowhere safe to land. I finally hit the ground and shattered.

These days when people ask me I say I am single, swiftly followed by "happily single" when I see sympathy wash across their faces. Is it so strange to find a woman my age who actively chooses her own company? Previous generations would have labeled me a spinster, destined to sit alone in my house with cats and regrets, but here at the beginning of the twenty-first century I know there's a swath of independent women living the same situation. I have neither cats nor regrets and most days no desire to change this situation—most days I relish it. But there is, I will admit, the occasional storm of longing that slams me to the ground when I least expect it, days when I'm tired of hearing about love, tired of reading about marriage and families and the unending monotony of the school run. There are days when I feel I am missing out, that I've stepped so far away from what's considered the norm I have excluded myself from the club. I have no problem with being alone—I thrive in my alone—but to call myself "single" suggests I am incomplete in some way, that living a deeply felt life by myself is not enough.

I've been casting around for a new way to define my contentedly single status, something strong and solid that captures how I support myself, emotionally, physically, mentally, and spiritually. I tried "family-of-one" for a while, but I could feel the barbs of lack poking my side, and though it felt close to where I am right now, what would happen if farther down the path I became a family of two, or four, or—heaven help me—more? And then it came to me: I am a *tribe of one*. A self-supporting, own-hand-holding cheer-leading squad of me.

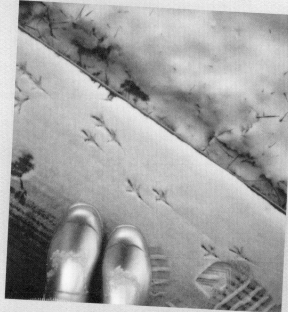

I've hiked the trails of my alone so thoroughly that if my world cracked open tomorrow I'd survive because I know how to look after myself, how to weather the storm when all I have is a broken umbrella. There are times in our lives when being a tribe of one is a necessity rather than a choice, when family live far away and friends are yet to be found. We can be a tribe of one within the loving arms of a relationship, we can let others into our tribe and hold hands to provide comfort and support. But it's this first tribe, this powerful, deeply rooted sense of self that will sustain us as we answer our calling, step through the trials of motherhood, or brave the disappointments and the inevitable loss of our loved ones. If we can hold our *own* hands we are never alone.

Like any new relationship there is awkwardness at first, maybe a little shyness, as you try yourself on for size. You know who to be when you're with your husband or mother or child, but who are you with yourself, when you don't have a role to play? Imagine what it would be like to spend some time one-on-one with the woman whose eye you so studiously avoid in the mirror—what would it be like to sit down with her and tell her how you feel? Maybe you'll discover how much fun she is to be around, you'll remember the things that make her belly laugh and how much she loves lying in the sun. Imagine you're a puzzle to be worked out—where would you start? How much would you share on a first date with yourself?

Solitude doesn't have to be a special month-long retreat from the world. It can be enjoyed in little pockets of time within our everyday lives—an afternoon in the park, a day on the sofa, a quiet weekend at home. On some of my most disconnected days I've sat down with a notebook and pen and asked, *How do I really feel today?* letting the words fall onto the page without censoring them. I've had divinely perfect moments of solitude in a bathtub, taking a whole hour to lie back and sink into my thoughts. I've spent nights in hotels with a few comforts from home—my favorite incense, my music, some herbal tea bags; I've traveled as far as the Rift Valley and eaten lunch by myself in a safari lodge, taking my coffee outside to sit in the long grass and stare at the African sky. Practicing the alone at home makes it so much easier to be out in the world by ourselves.

For some, the very thought of sitting quietly is like asking them to walk on nails. *There's too much to do. I don't have time to spend on me. Everyone else has to be looked after first.* The problem with putting everyone else first is you put yourself last, which may be absolutely necessary for a while, but eventually the woman in the mirror deserves some attention. *You are worth paying attention to.* Put the oxygen mask on first—let yourself breathe and be nourished and cared for, so you can do the same for the others in your life. Spending time with yourself is never wasted—it's an investment in your emotional health, and if we can be gentle and kind with ourselves, we can be gentle and kind with others.

One of the most powerful things I've ever done was to take myself out on dates. Having been in relationships my entire adult life, I wasn't used to doing certain things on my own, and the day I took myself to the cinema was a day to remember. I'd always thought that people who did this were sad lonely folk who had no friends. *I know,* what a horrible thing to think, but it came straight out of my own fears of being alone and friendless. I've since discovered that solo cinema trips are, in fact, one of the most delicious treats of all time. I buy something hot and calorific to drink, watch whatever film I want and sit wherever I like (without someone fidgeting beside me or kicking the back of my seat). I sink into the womb-like darkness of the auditorium and lose myself for a couple of hours on a rainy afternoon. It's pure bliss.

After discovering that joy, I got bolder: I tried a lunch on my own. And I don't mean a humble sandwich quickly eaten on a park bench. I'm talking about ordering a delicious lunch from a menu somewhere nice. I'm talking waiter service and a proper

check at the end. There is something incredibly empowering about taking yourself out for lunch; the first few times I felt awkward and ate quickly and left fast, but these days I like to sit and savor my space. I might bring a book, and sometimes I'll work on my laptop, but often there's nothing to hide behind—just me, my plate of food, a room full of people to watch and my thoughts to think. To be me . . . in public. I especially like dining alone while abroad—San Francisco and Montreal provided memorable opportunities to sit quietly and watch the world go by; I even refused the offer of a newspaper to read. Sometimes I'll get quizzical stares from the other patrons, but generally people are too wrapped up in their own world to notice me sitting there. I always share a secret smile with other women I see eating alone—maybe they're like me and dig the lone dining mission, or they're taking a break from work, or are mothers escaping their kids for an hour. I like being a member of the lone diners club—it feels decadent somehow, like a proud signal to the world that I'm not afraid to just be me.

Perhaps this all sounds rather obvious to you, if you've been self-dating for years. But if you fear, like I did, that doing this stuff alone is sad or, more likely, exposing and makes you feel vulnerable then I invite you to take yourself out on a date the next chance you get. Start with a matinee and a box of popcorn, and then work your way up to a lunch date. Take a book, find a cozy spot in the corner of the restaurant and see what happens. If nothing else, the feeling of accomplishment will keep you buzzing all the way home.

They say we must eat sensibly, exercise regularly, and take time out to de-stress—I'd like to add *fall in love with ourselves* to that list. To be able to cultivate our self-esteem and sense of worth we need to get to know ourselves—the soft tender places and the bold and powerful places. The hurts, the joys, and the successes. We are worth this nurturing time—we deserve it. With a little practice you'll soon be craving the alone times, no longer fearing the space to think, but searching for ways to eke out an hour here and a weekend there, creating pockets of space to dance in the warmth of your own inner light.

You are not as awful as you think you are.

You are amazing.

reflection

In *Journal of a Solitude,* May Sarton writes: "I don't know whether the inward work is achieving something or whether it is simply the autumn light, but I begin to see my way again, which means to resume *myself.*" Possibly the most important and valuable work you will ever do is to get to know yourself. Solitude wraps us in a blanket of time, holding us while we burrow deep inside. To truly know yourself, to be brave enough to sit in that space and sift through the silt of your life, is to create freedom. When you know you can rely on yourself, no matter what, you can do anything. Go anywhere. Make magic happen in your life, because you have an ally in your corner who'll always cheer you on. Who will believe in you and mop your brow before you head back out for round two.

You have YOU.

Before you take yourself on a date this week I want you to check in with yourself right now, in the silence of these pages. Turn off the television and the music. Switch off your phone and shut down the computer. Sit without speaking for a while. Listen to the hum of the fridge, the buzz of the lights. The rumble of the cars passing. The wind blowing against the windows. Hear the rhythms of life being lived on the other side of the walls.

Now, close your eyes and become aware of the melody of your breathing, noticing how the in breath is always followed by an out breath. *You breathe in, you breathe out.* Thoughts might dance around your head, but you still breathe in. And breathe out. Sit quietly for a while, bringing your hands together in your lap, one hand wrapping over the other. Hold your hands together gently but firmly, like you'd hold a child's hand. Feel the warmth growing between your palms and your fingers. Feel the strength in your hands, as you breathe in, and breathe out.

Keeping your attention in your hands, say the following words to yourself: *I'm here for you. I'm not letting go.* Say the words out loud, focusing on the warmth in your hands, knowing that the hands that hold yours right now will never go away. You are supported and you are loved.

Sit quietly for a little longer, feeling the warmth of those supportive hands.

And then when you are ready, open your eyes.

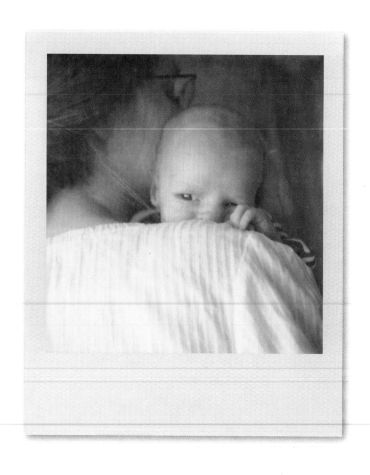

the art of belonging

"She is a friend of mind. She gather me, man. The pieces I am, she gather them and give them back to me in all the right order. It's good, you know, when you got a woman who is a friend of your mind."

—Toni Morrison, from *Beloved*

i t's three days after Christmas day and I'm missing my family, specifically a little boy called Noah. We've had the coldest December in one hundred years, yet today the snow is melting outside my window, revealing the streets in all their gray glory. I miss the snow, and I miss my nephew, and I wish it was Christmas Day again. It's been the first holiday season I've looked forward to in as long as I can remember, the new addition to our family bringing so much joy with him. There was no way the day would be anything less than sparkling. We filled it with just the right amount of food and laughter, the day paced by naps and feeding times. Noah wanted to feed himself and ate his Christmas dinner with his hands, yet another first we captured in photographs. My family doesn't have many traditions, but we always make sure we're together for birthdays and Christmas. I speak to my sister on the phone every day, and my mother once or twice a week, and in between e-mails are sent so we always know where each other is, something that even I appreciate, here in my cozy cave of alone.

The day my father left we became a family of three, a shape that's expanded and contracted to let others in over the years, but at its core we're a powerful trio, or we were until eight months ago, when I helped my sister push a new life into the world. The arrival of Noah has changed everything, both in the big obvious ways and the smallest most profound, and I don't know if I have ever seen my mother as happy as she is when she's sitting on the floor playing with her grandson. And though there's an ache inside me, knowing I may never give her a grandchild, I feel such warmth when I see her delight in Noah, appreciating how she must have loved us as kids when she wipes his face with a damp cloth. She shows him the garden as they stand at the window, and as I finish my toast I wonder if she did the same when I was a baby, holding me, kissing my head, showing me the snow. Seeing them together is like watching my childhood photos come alive.

I didn't know it was going to be like this. I had my fears at the beginning before Noah arrived. I don't know why it's so hard to remember that our fears rarely materialize, and that in bracing ourselves for the impact, we *create* the impact. If only we could let go and soften our bodies, soften our minds, soften our expectations, whatever happens would be felt as a nudge rather than a crash. I feared I would lose my sister to the cult of motherhood, and that I, the single childless one, would be left out in the cold, wrapping my tribe of one around me, my best friend lost to a club I couldn't join. My fears came from the abandoned girl, scared of being left on her own; the woman doubting her own fertility, or capability to be a mother. As my sister's pregnancy progressed I kept my thoughts in check as best I could, listening to her fears about the impending change, knowing she needed me more than ever. The day we discovered he was a boy I felt a genuine bubble of excitement in my stomach and began using the word *nephew*—it made me feel involved, that her pregnancy included me too somehow, a continuation of our entangled lives as sisters. But there was also an awareness that this was a rite of passage she would take alone, and it was my job to support and love her, but to also get out of her way. All my life I've been told to look after my sister; it's as natural as blinking to me, and with that sense of responsibility comes the expectation that I should always go first: I left home first, I fell in love first, I went to college first, and all the while my sister sought her path in the colossal shadow of the girl she just wanted to befriend, the girl who had other ideas about *that*. Little sisters are annoying until you're all grown up and realize she's been your best friend all along. Who else but my sister can remember the years after our father left? The confusion of that time is much easier to fathom when there are two perspectives to shine light on it. Even now we can talk of those years and discover a new thought, a new feeling, a new part of the blueprint to unpick and examine.

As the days stretched into a never-ending wait, the baby inside her womb stretched his legs, preparing to make his entrance into our lives. "You do realize you're going to be somebody's mummy," I said, the day before they induced her.

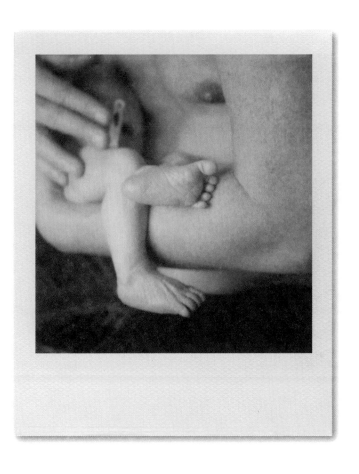

"I know, it's so weird," she said. "I've always been the little one."

The day of his birth is a story shared between my sister, her partner, and me, our mother waiting outside the ward, a twenty-six hour transition from before to after, the final ten-hour stretch fueled by laughing gas for my sister and endless sandwiches for me. As my sister drifted in and out of consciousness, I have never been more present than I was during those last few hours. I took photographs of the delivery room so she could remember the place where her son was born; I held her hand through the contractions; I stepped away to let the new father hold his son. I saw his little face come out, and watched the slippery smallness of his body carried up and over into my sister's arms. And I didn't know it at the time, but my heart opened right then in preparation for what was to come; if I'd listened closely I'd have heard the bandages rip.

After the euphoria of the birth came the emotional crash of the day after, my fears washing out of my eyes as my sister lay in hospital, learning the music of her son's cries. I've often wondered if perhaps those fears came from a darker place inside me, a childhood memory of the new baby coming home, my place in the order of things rearranged. Wherever it came from I felt ashamed of my sorrow, and returning to my alone was acutely painful, my own hormones battering me from within.

And then, as it often does on this amazing fairground ride, everything changed for the better. The healing began the first weekend I stayed over. Noah was a few weeks old, his parents sleep-deprived and giggly. I remember the exact moment I fell in love, holding him in my arms, standing by the same kitchen window. As I looked into his eyes, I had this incredible surge of recognition; he wasn't a stranger, he was family. I was overwhelmed with the urge to protect him; to smear mud on our faces and perform some kind of ritual, to celebrate the arrival of a long-lost brother. It was exhilarating and strange and beautiful. From then on I was a goner; just one sniff of his fuzzy little head left me in raptures. I've had wonderfully close relationships with friends' children, so I assumed, in my typically naive way, that this auntiehood gig would be the same. But this first tentative year of expansion and love has revealed that this time it's different. *He is family*, and the very word itself has taken on new meaning. He is a part of my sister, and because she is a part of me then *he* is a part of me too . . . it's a big mush of family connection, and I feel it with everything I am.

The family we are born into is life's greatest lottery, but they are not our only tribe. At our core most human beings wish to belong to something greater than themselves, dancing between our need for solitude and the desire to be where others are.

The family we are born into is life's greatest lottery, but they are not our only tribe. At our core most human beings wish to belong to something greater than themselves, dancing between our need for solitude and the desire to be where others are. We spend our days spinning through the orbits of our family, our neighbors, colleagues at work, and those nameless strangers we see every day. And then there are our friends, old and new. Some are friendships of convenience and circumstance; others are friends we inherit through our partners. And somewhere in that mixed bag we hope to find women who are our sisters under the skin. In the company of women I feel most like myself; I can count my male friends on one hand. In my relationships there were double dates and dinner parties, but in this bare bones time of just me, my reconnection to myself blooms in the company of other women.

Before bereavement forced me to rethink my life, I lived from a place of neediness and insecurity, my lack of self-love reflected back to me in my relationships. Not knowing my own worth, I looked for validation from the outside—in both my romantic partnerships and friendships. I needed my friends to value me, to make time exclusively for us when we were together. I now realize that I *needed* them to love me, to not leave me—sound familiar? The little abandoned girl inside me was making her needs known, filtering her emotions into every relationship I had. There's a definite correlation between the amount of trust we have in our friendships and the amount of self-worth we have in ourselves. Lacking self-worth tends to equal a needy friend, and there I was attaching expectations to my friendships, the controlling big-sister side of my personality fusing with the needy child and making an emotional mess. Some of my most dynamic friendships were borne out of mutual neediness, the two of us coming together at a time in our lives when we were both single and searching, or both heartbroken and moping, or climbing the career ladder and living the city life. Like really does attract like and I've been in my fair share of dysfunctional duos.

Writing all this down makes me cringe; no one wants to be seen as needy or controlling, and we rarely understand our actions at the time. By cultivating self-awareness we can uncover the truth about past behaviors, following the clues back to the source of the hurt. I lost a lot of friends after I crashed—some could not face me, while others I chose to drift away from. The more I healed the past, the more threatening I appeared to the friends who weren't ready to face their own demons. Losing a friend is painful whoever instigates the break, and I'm sure there are more elegant ways to end a friendship, but I've only ever been able to do it *really badly.* By trying to avoid the hurt and recriminations I back away and disappear, hoping my silence is explanation enough. So awful, so cowardly, but how do you tell someone you care about that you can't be in their life anymore, that you've grown apart and it's time to move on? I've been on the receiving end of this too, and I know how hurtful it can be, and yet, I have done it. We all have our reasons: self-preservation, fear, or maybe just knowing when it's time to get off the bus.

While my friendships were playing musical chairs, I sank into me. Lest you think all neediness and attachment was dropped overnight, it was a process that took three years, and is one I still tend to today. My emotions dictate my actions, which is why I start my days quietly, picking up the rhythm as I go along. In these quiet years I've learned that the friend I need most is inside me—this was the key that changed everything. Drawing strength from my own reserves—self care, quiet space, checking in through words and images—means I don't rely on anyone else to feel better; I take responsibility for my own needs. And when the hormonal winds disturb the calm, as they always do, I make myself sit with the discomfort—a twinge of envy, a crisis of faith—and feel it out. Chocolate medication helps too.

By learning how to navigate my sharp edges I can honor those parts in others. The friends who've since come into my life are all on similar journeys. And as we've shared our stories

I've discovered I'm much more able to hold a friendship lightly and not crush it with the force of my need—the need is simply no longer there. If our relationships truly are mirrors, then these women reflect the new me: the woman who finally sees that she has worth, who's learning patience and foresight, and still merrily swears like a sailor. Even friendships from before have been strengthened and renewed as a new level of honesty emerges between us—without the neediness, I'm able to tell the truth.

I've talked to people who find friendship daunting, who worry that by opening their lives to another they have a responsibility to be there for them, no matter what. That can be scary when you're only just keeping your own self together. Friendships between women in particular are expected to be nurturing, a safe space created for each woman to weave her tales of motherhood, responsibility, and whatever else is weighing heavy on her heart. How wonderful if this were always the case! What enriched lives we would lead if we could retreat inside these red tents with our confidants to cry and bond over our moon cups. So perhaps that's going a little too far, but I hope you see my point—there is always an ideal, and there is always the disappointment when the ideal looks different from how you thought. In my experiences of women coming together, I've been privy to joy, sisterhood, and, yes, lots of tears of recognition, but I have also witnessed jealousy, competitiveness, and drama queens. When agendas and egos clash, diplomacy goes out the window, and suddenly someone is "standing in their power" and demanding to "speak their truth" and everyone else is feeling awkward. There is wisdom in knowing when to retreat, when to pull back from an energy that drains you and to protect yourself, because sharing ourselves—our true, messy, vulnerable selves—requires incredible courage, letting another person see who we really are. We want to appear to have it all together, even when we don't, but if we can let go of our expectations, and remember that we all feel shy and uncertain at times, we can hold a space for our friendships to grow, to lend support and nonjudgmental ears, bring pizza and beer when needed, and be a sounding board for secret dreams. Cultivate the friendships that make you feel more yourself, without apology or explanation. Reach out when you need support and pull back when you need space.

The more I excavate myself, the richer my relationships with others become, because as we connect with our true selves we have so much more to give. By appreciating our own company we're reminded why others might want to spend time with us; that we have gifts to offer, kindness. No more pretending. No more avoiding. No more being anything other than exactly who we are.

So how to find these sisters under the skin? Working from home maxed out my friendship credit line, so my community came to me via my computer screen. Fifteen years ago this wouldn't have been possible but the Internet has facilitated the greatest social club of all time, where writing a blog is like pinning an ad on a global notice board, attracting like-minded people who feel a connection to your words. My blog began as a simple space to share my passions and talk about my days. There was no great plan and it certainly wasn't my intention to write extensively about my grief, but as I became more comfortable sharing my feelings online, the healing path wasn't far behind. Blogging gave me back my voice after a year of feeling mute, the daily writing a way to measure my progress, the support from my readers such a boon on the days I crumbled, a collective cheer on the days I soared. I felt seen again, that I had a purpose, that my story was helping others, while they in turn helped me.

Blogging is a two-way activity. While sharing my thoughts online I also explored the blogs of others and many nights were spent reading back through the archives of new finds, feeling a connection to the author and reaching out with a comment or e-mail. Getting to know someone in this way—virtually,

without any physical contact—is curious at first, but a lot of emotional ground can be covered in e-mails and phone calls. As we'd shared so much already via our blogs, we cut through the crap and got straight to the truth—the women who'd endured similar grief experiences were particularly forthright, an easy and immediate honesty between us from the very first contact, such a blessing after a year in almost total seclusion.

So this is how I gathered friends from all over the world; some I've met in person on trips, others have visited me in England, and many more remain valued supporters from the virtual sidelines. And I realize I've just painted a dreamy picture of blogging, one that's maybe verging into *red tent* territory, so let me back up and say that, yes, there are also charlatans and trolls out there in the online world, but luckily they are in the minority. In my six years of blogging I've received only three mean-spirited comments (which I still remember word-for-word) but they haven't deterred me from sharing the way I do. Remember, *you* are the queen of your online domain and *you* have the power to delete at will.

It can feel intimidating starting a blog when there are so many others clamoring for attention online, but just like any other party, all you need do is find your corner, get comfortable, and start making conversation. At first you'll feel like you're talking to yourself, but eventually people will stop by as you reach out to other bloggers and start building connections. People like to cluster together in like-minded groups online, mirroring our off-line desire to belong to a tribe, so it's not uncommon to feel on the outside at first, wishing to be let in. The phenomenon of the popular girl in high school is alive and well in the blogosphere and inevitably you'll find the blogs that push your buttons. People write blogs for many different reasons, yet everyone, even those purporting to be sharing the most intimate details of their lives, is sharing the edited version they feel comfortable putting out into the world—the *PR version,* if you like. I have a friend who writes about life with her kids in the English countryside, a dreamy mix of home baking, camping, and fishing along the river.

"If I had kids I'd want your life," I told her. "Your blog always looks so cozy."

"God, I wish I had that life too," she laughed. "You should see the piles of laundry I keep out of sight!"

So if readers ever feel inadequate when faced with her *Mother of the Year* lifestyle, they should know she's wishing for that life too. By fashioning it online she's manifesting her dream, and while the homemade cakes are integral to how she's raising her kids, my friend chooses to carefully edit out the less pretty parts, like the money worries and leaking roof. And I can understand—it feels empowering to show our best side to the world. Who wants to look like they're struggling when everyone else seems to be doing just fine? But as my friend has discovered whenever she's shared a heartfelt post about the less shiny side of life, people appreciate honesty. Anything written from the heart reminds us that even if it looks like we're gliding gracefully down the river, below the surface we're all paddling frantically.

I like stories that get to the marrow of life, the hard and the truthful and the real. The tales of living that make me sit up and shout, "Yes, I feel that too!" It can be hard to meet like-minded people in our off-line lives, and so easy to feel isolated when no one seems to share our passions. This is why dipping a toe in the blogosphere is worth the risk, to find *your* people. Tell us about your dreams and which flavor ice cream you prefer. Tell us about your first kiss or the day you rode your bike to the sea. Share a photograph of your smiling face, and reach out to the people you'd like to know better, who love the color chartreuse and drink their coffee the same way as you. I believe in blogging from the heart, so let's dig in to what matters and send a siren call out to the world.

Here I am.
Let's play!

reflection

I was so nervous the day I met my first online friend in person. We'd already chatted on the phone and sent e-mails galore, so I knew we'd have lots to talk about. You get a sense of a person when you read their blog, but it's another story when you're sitting face-to-face. But as it turned out, we had a lovely afternoon and made plans to meet again. When we said good-bye, I asked if I was what she'd expected after reading my blog, and she smiled and said, "Absolutely. But you swear more."

We are still good friends to this day.

Building a friendship requires a certain degree of vulnerability right from the start. Just like in any courtship, we reveal pieces of ourselves as we feel more comfortable, sharing our past and hopes for the future, our opinions and occupations. Letting others see who we are so they, in turn, feel safe revealing themselves to us. In many ways opening up online is easier—there's no awkward eye contact to navigate, no uncomfortable silences after we've spilled the beans. We can choose our words with care, sharing our thoughts far more articulately than if we were to speak to them in person.

Open a new blog post or document on your computer and write down the following headline: Ten things you might not know about me.

Compile ten juicy tidbits about yourself that you've yet to share online. Consider the quirky parts of your personality that make you *you*: know how to build a motorcycle from scratch? Got a tattoo on your foot? Try pushing against your comfort zone a little, spilling a few beans that make you squirm alongside other fun facts about yourself.

In my second month of blogging I first published my own bean-spilling post. My tenth bean was as follows:

10. Thirteen months ago the man I loved died from a heart attack. My grief journey has brought me to this point, where I feel strong enough to reconnect with the world, and this blog is my attempt to honor the new person I have become.

It was the first time I'd revealed my situation on my blog and it felt good to finally put it out there.

If you don't have a blog yet, consider e-mailing your list to anyone in your life you'd like to get closer to. Start your e-mail with a heart-felt note explaining that you've completed an exercise in a book and wanted to share the results with people you cared about. Then invite them to do the same—you never know what worthwhile conversations it could start . . . .

Be brave and let yourself be seen.

unraveled

"The bad news is you're falling through the air, nothing to hang on to, no parachute. The good news is there's no ground."
—Chogyam Trungpa Rinpoche

i t's the first day of 2007 and I'm sitting at my desk creating a new blog for my photographs. Not quite ready to share my full name on the Internet, I'm racking my brain for a suitable alternative when a song starts playing on my computer. There, in the midst of beautifully sung lyrics, I hear my word—*unraveling*. The room doesn't get brighter, and I certainly don't levitate out of my chair, but I do feel a sense of *rightness*, like hearing that first click when you unlock a door. *Yes, that's the perfect word! I've been unraveling myself and the world around me.*

Despite my unraveling being borne out of the worst kind of situation, I didn't feel broken—on the contrary, I was wide open and more fully myself than I'd ever been before. The tangles of so many years of hurt were now undone, layers of old personalities and *should-bes* sloughed off until all that was left were the essential parts of me. With the benefit of hindsight I know finding the name for my photography and life was an important moment on my path; at the time I just thought I'd found an apt word, not knowing how far that one little word would take me. Our lives are not lived in a straight line; the choices and decisions we make take us in many directions, the crashes and collisions shunting us off our paths until we pick up the breadcrumb trail and get back on our way. We only ever recognize our big turning points in reverse—the weddings and divorces are obvious, but it's those smaller decisions, the ones that were made with a shrug, that can divert the course of our entire lives without us even knowing. If we knew something important had just occurred, would we still make the same decision? If we knew our world was about to change—maybe not in that moment, but somewhere down the line, when the chain of events we'd triggered finally came into being—would we feel excitement or fear? The butterfly effect of my own actions, felt years later, sitting in a cafe tracing the path backwards to the day a song started playing as I sat grappling with html in my pajamas.

I don't believe in luck but I do believe in listening intently to my gut, trusting that I know the answers even when I haven't a clue what the questions are. I have varying degrees of success with this method, but a perfect record of things going wrong when I ignore my intuition. I'm learning to distinguish between a reaction based in fear and one based in truth—the fear manifests as neediness, the conviction that I must do something, or see someone, or be somewhere, in case I miss out or lose an opportunity. Doing things I feel I *should* do, rather than want to do. But when I let myself be quiet, and get a sense of what I'm really feeling, I usually discover a very different answer. This works well for business decisions as well as personal ones—I'm getting good at saying no to the wrong things and practicing saying yes to the right.

It's been a long period of navel-gazing in the best possible way, clearing out the crap that cluttered up my path: the anger, the guilt, the need, and the doubt. There are still plenty of boxes I could clear out; this unraveling business is a lifetime endeavor, and now I'm on this path I have no desire to get off. One of the gifts of my bereavement was the enforced stillness, giving me time to reconsider every part of my life. I was fragile at first, but growing in strength with every trip to the supermarket, every morning I woke wanting to write. As I couldn't go back to my old life in the city, I needed to find a new way to pay the rent, surviving on credit cards and assistance from the government while I healed, my debt growing every day. It's hard to decipher your true passion when credit companies are hounding you every week—I've lost count of how many times my card was refused in a store. I was a photographer without a client and a writer without a commission. I could've spent three more years in therapy, but my wings were thrashing against the cage bars—it was time to fly. Time to find work. Time to prove to myself I could exist in the world without support. So I borrowed the money and moved to a new city where nobody knew me.

I flew.

And then I crash landed, temporarily.

All I can tell you is my gut made me do it. Somewhere underneath the panic about money, hiding among the fear of failure, I knew it was time to move on, that by continuing to live in my cave by the sea I'd never regrow that final layer of skin to cover my new bones. This time the turning point was

unmistakable, replete with flashing lights and a line of can-can dancers. I was ready to jump, and as I built myself up to launch into the air, I pushed down my anxieties—this was the right thing to do! I've rarely been so certain about anything, and that certainty fueled the move to Bath.

If we knew something important had just occurred, would we still make the same decision?

That first morning in a new city I woke barely able to move my limbs, my head screaming *WHAT HAVE I DONE* as I surveyed the boxes, the stove that didn't work, and the stained carpet—why hadn't I seen these before? The first month was brutal. With the training wheels off I wobbled and fell, the safe places gone: my home, my sea. I cried for two weeks straight, distraughtly calling my family, something I hadn't done since the early days of my bereavement. I'd thrust myself back out into the world, and it was unfamiliar and scary—I pined for my old home, for the lost connection to my love.

We're so quick to forget what nourishes us when we're distressed—it was two weeks before I thought to pick up my camera, venturing out to find the post office one day, the bank the next, small missions that gave me purpose and a way to learn the rhythm of the streets. Those early photographs remind me how displaced I felt, focusing in on the little details before I could take in the whole—I befriended the city, one frame at a time. It was during an early photo walk that I found my cafe to sit in and write. It felt safe there, surrounded by the mothers with their strollers and the rowdy groups of kids letting off steam. It became my daily pilgrimage to get me out of the house—every afternoon I bought a caramel latte and settled into the chair, plugged in my headphones and connected back to myself through my notebook. I spent hours nursing that single coffee, observing the people around me before turning back to the page. What began as short gratitude lists soon morphed into longer diary entries asking the right questions— *What's the point of all this unraveling if I can't pay my electric bill? Why is this so hard? How can I find a job?*

If you ask enough questions, the answers will filter through, and having a pen in your hand helps when they do—the trick is to sit down and ask. When we're living through a time of change, we tend to react first and consider later. Our heads fill with panic, our hearts beat faster, we tense up and want to run and hide. Living at the edge of our emotions like this leaves little room for rational thought. By creating some space physically—out of the house, away from the triggers—and mentally—soothing music on headphones, a blank page ready to be filled—we are better able to calm down and figure out what we need to do.

Slow down.

Create space.

Listen in.

slow down

create space

listen in

For me, the anxiety of not being able to support myself financially collided with the shock of being back out in the world. Without the safety net of family and therapist close by the panic started to grow. Even though I was still sure I had made the right move, I just wasn't convinced it was going to play out. My daily trawl through the newspaper for jobs was dispiriting, the employment agencies not much better. With so much competition for the few jobs that were out there, I found I was either ridiculously over-qualified or lacking in experience. I landed a few days' work at a portrait studio, which helped to bolster my confidence, but the frustration I felt fed the negative thoughts—*I have no money. I can't make all the rent this month. I'm screwed.* It was during a writing marathon one afternoon that it occurred to me that my thoughts were sabotaging my life, that I was so invested in them being The Truth there was no room for anything else. I hadn't created any space for possibility; I'd moved to a new city but I was still carrying old patterns. And because I was so very tired of feeling anxious I decided to try changing my thinking—not just as an abstract idea that sounded sensible, but an actual daily exercise I'd throw all my energy into. I started by writing out what I wanted in my life and—more crucially—how I wanted to *feel* every day.

I want to feel calm. I want some peace of mind. Security.
Independence. Possibility. I want to know the bills are taken care of.
I want to feel more powerful. I want to feel more focused.

What can I do to feel more powerful right now?

I can commit to a routine to feel more in control of my days. I can find
my wheels and get more done. It's time to take charge of my destiny
instead of crossing my fingers.

What can I do to feel more independent?

I can go to new places on my own—art galleries, coffee shops, local
events.

I can walk around the city with my cameras—keep my eyes open and
pay attention.

I can get more organized—unpack the last boxes, start planning meals.

What can I do to feel more focused?

I can be ready—shower first thing, eat regular meals, get some early
nights and early mornings.

Get the crap out of my head with daily journaling—get accountable
on this page.

Read my inspiring books—look for the clues.

Do more brainstorming.

Plan ahead.

I wrote this page in October 2008. Four months later I had manifested a creative business that is not only still supporting me but also flourishing.

How did I do it? It started with the realization that a lifetime of thinking pessimistically hadn't worked. Depression has been a constant throughout my life and with it comes the glass-half-empty disposition that was feeding my fear. But I'd known it was time to jump. I'd positioned myself in a new city that could hold the new life I wanted to build—now it was time to take my courage in my hands and *try*. After years of living at the whims of my right brain, I got practical. Every day I made a conscious effort to rewire my thinking, shifting my thoughts from lethargy and fear to being proactive and having hope. Every time the negative story started playing I countered with repeated affirmations and constantly examined what I was thinking. As a chronic PMS sufferer, this wasn't always easy, but my new environment helped me focus because nothing around me was familiar, nothing carried old stories to trip me up.

Before I continue, let me talk a little more about affirmations. I've read enough metaphysical and self-help books over the years to be familiar with the vernacular that's used. I keep a metaphorical bag of salt in my pocket so I can take a pinch whenever I come across an idea or instruction that has a whiff of rainbows and unicorns about it. The word *affirmation* has

always made me cringe but I was so desperate to bring change into my life I was willing to try anything. In my mind I exchanged the word affirmation for *new words,* a small reframe that helped me get past my skepticism and become open to possibility, one of the desired feelings I'd identified in my journaling. The *new words* I used were: *I have unlimited abundance.* "Abundance" encompassed everything I wished to bring into my life, not just financial abundance, but new relationships, connections, joy, and opportunity. I imagined how abundance would feel, from buying gifts for my family and traveling abroad to writing every day and collaborating with inspiring people. I said my *new words* as if they were already fact, as if the abundance and connection I longed for in my life were already my reality.

Years of journaling had taught me to find a quiet spot and be kind to myself to coax the words out. I knew to trust my instincts, now they weren't sending me mixed messages, now I'd let the little girl have a say in how I moved through the world. I changed my environment, getting out in the fresh air and away from the house—being at home let the crazies come out, while being outside distracted me, just as walks by the sea had been soothing years before. And when I was feeling doubtful and wished I could go back in time, I stayed present to my emotions and gave myself a break. *Hot bath, early night, I'm doing the best I can.*

Perhaps it was a coincidence that my circumstances changed. Just as I couldn't explain the feathers, I do sense that there is more in this world than we can see or understand. And I believe that we have more power to influence the course of our lives than we think we do, beyond making decisions about what to have for dinner. Whatever it was, it worked, and I felt like I was *participating* in my future prosperity, rather than standing by hoping for scraps.

My first three months in Bath were spent looking for a job and working just as hard toward the internal changes I wanted to achieve. By continually shifting my thoughts away from the negative I started noticing the clues. It was in this state of being open to possibility that I began to create my evening class. I'd moved knowing I had an offer to teach, but since the money I'd earn wasn't enough to buy a week's groceries I hadn't put it on my list of potential jobs. Now I was excited to try something new. Reading back through my journals, I sketched out a lesson plan, connecting the dots between what I'd done and what had worked. Such powerful change had occurred when I'd started to take self-portraits; I hoped to create something similar for my students. It felt like a daring experiment, and I was scared and excited—could I really guide women through a healing process using a *camera?* My inner critic was merciless in her mocking: *Who do you think you are? You'll embarrass yourself. They'll all ask for their money back.*

For the second time that year, I jumped without a net. On the first day I was full of nerves, going over and over my notes to make sure I had enough material to fill my two-hour class. And then something amazing happened—within five minutes of the class starting all my nerves left my body and I felt incredibly *calm.* As I introduced myself to the gathered women and explained the plan for class, I felt in control. I felt capable and whole, as if I'd led the class hundreds of times before. It was uncanny, and such a relief. As the weeks progressed I still felt nervous before each lesson, but by the end of the night I was soaring, high on the energy of facilitating work that not only seemed to be helping my students but was also repairing a deep wound in me—everything I'd been through, everything I'd faced, was helping someone else too. It's only now, three years later, that I see how healing that really was.

Finding work we love seems impossible when we're stuck in a job that doesn't fit us. I had plenty of false starts over the years: the photography business that crashed and burned, the freelance journalism I couldn't sustain after my bereavement. I've been a fashion editor, a telemarketer, and even served breakfast to hungry men at an oil refinery, but even when I was

doing work that should have been fulfilling, it wasn't. I worked hard but I wasn't happy; I'd get so far up the career ladder then run out of steam, my heart not in it any more. Now I realize I was chasing after goals that weren't fully aligned with what was important to me, but back then I didn't know this—I didn't know myself. The pattern of getting so far and then stopping carried on through my twenties and into my thirties—all I'd ever wanted was to wake in the morning and be excited to go to work. It seemed an impossible, and self-indulgent, dream.

My number one goal when I moved to Bath was to find meaningful work; it turned out I'd been in training for it all along. I was on the right path thinking photography was my vocation, but it wasn't in the shape I'd expected. I read an article that posed the following question: *What would you do every day, even if you weren't getting paid?* I knew the answer immediately because I was doing it already: I'd write my blog. I'd share photos with my online community and keep writing about my quest to live bravely and truthfully, no matter what. So when a friend suggested I teach my evening class online because she couldn't make it on Tuesday nights, I had my proverbial lightbulb moment. I knew of only one other person in my online circle who'd done something similar, and wasn't even sure if online classes could work, but the ideas were sparking faster than I could write them down. It took two months to restructure the course, build a simple website, and make preparations to share it with the world. On launch day I was so full of nerves I had to meet my sister for lunch. "Even if only ten women sign up for the class," I confided quietly, "that would be amazing." By the time I went to bed that night I had twenty enrollees; by the end of the first week I had one hundred. I was humbled that so many women were willing to take a chance on my course. Even when the class sold out the second time I ran it I was still amazed by how smoothly the work came together. I was doing something I felt passionate about, and there was an ease attached to it I hadn't experienced before. It wasn't so much being in the right place at the right time, but rather moving toward that which came naturally to me. And maybe the planets aligned too, just this once.

By the end of the first year I was supporting myself solely through the online classes. Despite years working as a free-lancer in London, I'd never considered myself business-minded, so from the start I wanted to weave the work that was important to me with business practices that felt genuine and transparent. I bought business books and scoured marketing websites, and while I read much that was useful, I knew the best way to promote my work was to just be myself. The audience that had grown around my blog had really connected to my story, and I wanted to honor their discernment and leave out the clever marketing tricks. Turns out all you really need is

a blog, a mailing list, and genuine excitement for your work. After so many years of false starts and disappointments I threw myself into building my business.

I'm very proud to be supporting myself as a tribe of one, and often think of the artist I met at that party all those years ago. When she described her work as her *rock* I felt a pang of envy, and now I understand how deeply I've wanted to find work that was more than just a way to pay the rent. The work we do can define us, can give us purpose. It can be a safe place when our personal lives are falling apart or it can feel like prison when we yearn to get back to our families. We spend more time at work than anywhere else, so it's no wonder so many of us crave work that brings meaning into our lives, that speaks to us on a soul level.

Turning our passions into a job does not always work out (as my failed portrait business had proven several years earlier) and not everyone wants to do their passion full-time. For some they remain wonderful pastimes that bring joy and fulfillment exactly as they are. But for those of us who are dissatisfied with our day jobs and feel called to find work that reflects our true interests, the clues to achieving this are already in our lives—we just need to know where to look for them.

The first clue is how you spend your spare time away from your day job. Do your interests involve volunteering or travel?

Do you like to make things? Are you a member of any societies? Do you like to be out in nature or working on projects at home? What books and magazines do you buy? *What would you do every day, even if you weren't getting paid?* Sometimes our passions are not obvious, so pay attention to what you *do* rather than what you *say*. If you're not sure where your true passions lie, or feel you have too many, think about the interests you had as a child—what did you want to be when you grew up? Is there anything in your life now that reflects those early dreams?

When was the last time you were really excited about something?

Next, think about where your true talents lie. What comes easily to you? What are you good at? It might be organizing gatherings and managing people or maybe you're the next Nigella Lawson in the kitchen. Do you have a knack for color coordination, or are you the dog whisperer in your family? What do your friends ask you to help them with? What have you always had a flare for?

Be sure to consider the difference between the pastimes you enjoy and the skills you have a true aptitude for. For example, I've always enjoyed painting and am in awe of artists who draw from their imaginations, but while playing with paints and canvas is fun once in a while, I know my true talents lie elsewhere. I could learn to paint better, but it doesn't come naturally to me. Taking well-composed and evocative photographs, on the other hand, has always been my gift. True talents can be honed and expanded but from the very beginning there's an ease threaded through them. My sister is a gifted illustrator and teacher, and whenever I've seen her teach I'm impressed by how she wrangles a room full of art students, opening their heads and shining a light inside. I, on the other hand, teach best online, using images and writing to inspire, connect, and create community. When we find the right forum for our true talents, synapses spark and ideas solidify.

Think about where your true talents intersect with how you spend your time. Where's the sweet spot for you? When my courses took off it became clear how my hobby—blogging and online socializing—and my true talent—photography—melded so well together. I'd been creating the pathway to work I was passionate about, unbeknown to me.

The final factors to consider are the community and connections you have around you, and how you inhabit that world. If we hope to be paid for the work we do it can't be done in a vacuum; at some point other people will need to get involved. At its most basic, work is giving our time, services, or goods in exchange for money from an employer, client, or customer. If the skills you have mean you'll be making a product then you're in search of customers; if you offer a service, you need to find clients. It may be that your true talents are best shared with an employer, but no matter whether you're selling goods or your time, other people are necessary.

As an introverted soul, I like the relative privacy my online business gives me, despite seemingly being "out there" all the time. Working from home is perfect for me but a more extroverted person would likely find it isolating. What suits your personality? Working for ourselves brings a sense of freedom into our lives, but it can also get lonely—do you work better with a partner or a team? Who can you reach out to in your community right now?

I've only touched on a few possibilities in the space I have here, but whether you're in between jobs, craving change, going back to work after a period away or just sure that you were meant for something more, the best place to start is within, unraveling the dreams that call to you when you close your eyes. And of course, not everyone wants to change jobs, but having spent time with my community, both off- and online, I know that if you're creatively inclined and feel drawn to the thoughts in this book, you most likely yearn to express your authentic self in all you do. It's a desire that touches all parts of our lives, from our relationships with our family and friends, to our work, beliefs, and even the place we live. It doesn't surprise me that the years I struggled with my working life were also the years I was the least connected to myself. And this is why we unravel—to heal the hurts of the past so we can move forward unencumbered by the baggage that's kept us small; to heal the hurts of the present so we live each day with intention and awareness; and to know how to heal the future hurts when they happen, because they will and we'll be ready.

I believe that by being the best and most healed version of ourselves we can truly make a difference in the world. I'm not an activist or politician, and I'm not able to have any direct impact on the areas of the world where help is needed. But what I *can* do is make a difference in the small pocket of the world I call home. I can live with integrity and be honest about my feelings, even when they hurt. I can put my whole heart into my work and pay forward the generosity that was shown to me when my world fell apart. I can look after myself, knowing that by healing my own hurts I won't be passing them on to anyone else. In a society like ours, filled with so many emotionally wounded people acting out their pain, this is possibly the most important work we could ever do—*heal our hurts so we don't pass them on*.

Are you ready to try?
Let's do this.

reflection

"Success means having the courage, the determination and the will to become the person you believe you were meant to be."
—GEORGE SHEEHAN

I like this quote very much. I especially like that Sheehan doesn't say, "Success means earning more than your neighbor." Or, "Success means finishing first every time." No, success means having the *courage* to become the person you *believe you were meant to be* . . . in whatever shape that takes for you. I watch my sister as she becomes the mother she was meant to be, fierce and brave and giving. I watch my friends as they peel back the layers of themselves, stepping away from jobs and relationships that no longer fit them. It takes guts to appraise our lives with honest eyes, to get quiet enough to hear the truth that waits patiently for our attention. True personal success has nothing to do with money, cars, or vacations; it's about living every day of our lives with as much integrity as we can muster. It's about going to bed knowing we've done the best we can, even on the bad days. Especially then.

I'd like to introduce you to someone important.

First, find a space in your home where you won't be interrupted for the next fifteen minutes or so. Sit comfortably in front of a mirror, one where you can see your whole head and shoulders. Close your eyes and take three deep breaths, in through your nose and out through your mouth . . . s l o w l y. As you inhale imagine yourself being filled up with calm and quiet; as you exhale imagine all the tensions of the day being released from your body. Now, open your eyes and look into the mirror, taking the time to regard each of your facial features in turn, without judgment . . . your hair . . . forehead . . . eyebrows . . . eyes . . . nose . . . mouth . . . your neck . . . your whole face. Practice looking with kind eyes, as if you were looking at the face of a person you love: your child or sibling, spouse or best friend.

When you feel ready, try *smiling* at the person you see in the mirror. It doesn't have to be a huge grin—start with a small smile, a little acknowledgment that you see the woman looking back at you.

For the next seven days, try smiling at yourself whenever you catch your eye in a mirror. It might feel silly at first. It might feel uncomfortable. But she is your ally and has been waiting for you.

It's time to say hello.

epilogue

Sometimes it takes darkness and the sweet
confinement of your aloneness
to learn

anything or anyone
that does not bring you alive

is too small for you.
—David Whyte, from his poem, "Sweet Darkness," 2007

Today is the sixth anniversary of his death and I'm spending the day quietly writing. The living room is bursting with
sunlight and I've pulled the curtains across to stop the light
catching my laptop screen and blinding me. I'm really not
complaining, though. When I went out for bread this morning I
noticed snowdrops and crocuses had sprung up in the church-
yard; spring is on her way at last and I'm counting down the
days till the magnolia trees are in bloom again. If there were
any cobwebs of sadness when I woke they've been swept out
by the promise of warmer days to come. I don't miss him like I
used to; I still have my moments when I'll think of something

he said, or remember the way he'd smile before kissing me, but even that happens less these days. He is a treasured memory from another lifetime, and I'm so grateful for everything that has come into my life since that it's hard to think of the grief I felt as anything but a gift. Today of all days I understand how far I have come.

The phone rings—it's my sister.

"You'll never guess what happened," she says.

"What? Did he walk?!"

"Yes! It happened last night. He was leaning against the sofa, facing Mum, and she put her arms out to him and said 'Come on, then' and he took two steps toward her! Wait—How did you know?"

So the smallest person in my life has taken his first wobbly steps, and it's not lost on me that I hear about it on such a significant day. It's as if he knew exactly the right time to be brave and give it a try, convincing me yet again that this little boy is here to mend all our hearts. Noah is the most alive person I know, exploring the world with his fingers and taste buds, his mouth like a third hand as he chews and drools his way through new objects, new toys, a bit of cat food here, a dirty tissue there. He devours new experiences fearlessly, and everything is equal—there's no better book to chew, no difference between a slipper and a laptop, they're all fair game. He inspires me to be brave and take my first wobbly steps toward love, toward a more expanded life, even if I might fall down.

I didn't know any of this was going to happen. Which is a pretty silly thing to say, really—who does know what's going to

happen, other than when we concoct plans for ourselves to try and make out like we have some control over our lives. The longer I'm alive, the more I know that this is a fantasy. Bereavement taught me that one day life is one shape, and the next it might be another, without warning, explanation, or recourse. Even now I have the urge to swaddle my loved ones in bubble wrap to keep them safe, but I know that's impossible. I can decide what to eat for lunch but I have no say over a hard drive crashing, a loved one dying, or a cell turning malignant—so much is out of my control. When I truly accept that, when I remind myself to live today and trust that tomorrow will take care of itself, I find I can breathe a little easier.

I hope this book has been helpful, that you have found a thread or two to begin your own unraveling journey. We tend to look for the *whys* when bad things happen—*Why did this happen to me? What did I do to deserve this?* But if we can reframe it, we can take back the power—*How can I make this better? How is this making me stronger?* The answers don't come immediately, but they will come when you're ready to hear them. We are here to experience life as thoroughly and truthfully as we can, to tell our stories to one another and share what we know; to be proud of our dreams and our perfectly imperfect selves. By sharing our stories we feel less alone, so I send my story out into the world in the hope that it reaches the hands of those who need it.

The Real Me

I am unashamedly gloriously imperfect.
I fail more than I win.
I still struggle to get yoga, no matter how hard I try.
I eat when I'm feeling lonely
and have replaced cigarettes with food.
I'm impatient and disapproving.
I'm far too opinionated.
I'll go to great lengths to hide my double chin from you.
I beat myself up, often.
I have days when all I want to do is lie down on the sofa.
I often forget to brush my teeth.
I hate shaving my legs,
And I'd rather eat pizza than drink a wheatgrass shot.
But who wouldn't?
I don't always love myself.
I swear too bloody much.
But I'm doing the best I can.
I make people laugh.
I tell it like it is.
I really don't know how to lie.
I have big dreams
and I love kissing.

I walked through fire and survived.
I'm learning how to forgive myself.
I see what others might miss.
I am an auntie, a daughter, a sister, and a friend.
I am healed and whole again.
There's no need to hide anymore,
so here I am.
It's nice to meet you.

book friends

I may have already mentioned this, but I love books. *Books are our friends.* Whenever anything happens in my life my first instinct is to find the book that will solve/cure/explain the mystery. So here are a few of the book friends who've supported me over the last few years and continue to do so to this day.

Grief

Out of the twenty or so books on grief I read, there were two that spoke to me more viscerally than the others. The first was *Companion Through the Darkness,* a collection of essays and diary excerpts Stephanie Ericsson wrote after her husband died of a heart attack. At the time she was pregnant with their first child. Ericsson reassured me that I wasn't mad to spend all night staring into space and all day crying. I wasn't mad to not want to talk to another soul for weeks on end, and to beat myself up with survivor's guilt. As she voiced her anger, inertia, and despair, I knew someone else had felt what I was feeling, and that they'd survived. Her words were a map I could follow—consolation when I needed it, a trigger at other times. I kept her book beside my bed for two whole years.

When I first read Joan Didion's *The Year of Magical Thinking,* I lost count of how many times I had to put the book down and sob. Though my relationship with my partner was so very different from her marriage to John, I found my own experience in her descriptions of the *strangeness* of grief—the magical thinking we encounter.

Poetry

In this book I've tried to describe how important poetry is to me, but you really need to read some to know why I love it so.

Start with Sharon Olds's *Selected Poems* (this is the book I asked her to sign) then dip into Erica Jong's *Becoming Light* (read "The Long Tunnel of Wanting You" and "Beast, Book, Body"). Next, let David Whyte weave his magic for you (if I had to choose an anthem, "Sweet Darkness" would be it). Li-Young Lee and his elegant poetry will soothe you ("Echo and Shadow" and "Persimmons" are two of my favorites). I fell so completely in love with *Rapture*, Carol Ann Duffy's achingly beautiful collection of poems, I bought a copy for each of my friends.

For other poetic gems, you can't go wrong investing in anything by the following poets (my favorite poems noted in parentheses): Naomi Shihab Nye ("Kindness"), Mary Oliver ("Wild Geese" and "When Death Comes"), Maya Angelou ("And Still I Rise"), Donna Masini ("Slowly"), Kim Addonizio ("For Desire"), and Marie Howe ("Death, the Last Visit").

Escapism

The fiction I read was filled with yearning—try reading Daphne Du Maurier's *Rebecca*, Charlotte Brontë's *Jane Eyre*, and *The Time Traveler's Wife* by Audrey Niffenegger back-to-back and not be in pieces by the end. The latter in particular was not only enjoyable but also hugely cathartic—the last scene broke me open so emphatically, I'm scared to read the book again.

I savored Jeanette Winterson's prose long into the night and highly recommend *Written on the Body*, *The Powerbook*, and *Sexing the Cherry*. *The English Patient* by Michael Ondaatje and *The Hours* by Michael Cunningham also made me swoon and are now dog-eared favorites.

I had countless epiphanies while reading *The Dance* by Oriah, *Women Who Run With the Wolves* by Clarissa Pinkola Estes, and *Journal of a Solitude* by May Sarton. These books were exactly what I needed to read at the time and they continue to inspire and console me like three old friends.

Writing

Really, it was Julia Cameron's *The Artist's Way* that started all this, arriving in my life at just the right time. No collection of writing books would be complete without *Bird by Bird* by Anne Lamott and *Writing Down the Bones* by Natalie Goldberg—both are essential reading for writers and artists alike. Steven Pressfield's *The War of Art* kicked my ass sufficiently to get started on this book. And *Chapter After Chapter* by Heather Sellers supported me when I wanted to throw my laptop out the window.

Photography

My photographic inspirations are always evolving, but some constants over the years include Diane Arbus, Dorothea Lange,

Francesca Woodman, and Uta Barth. I recently discovered the work of Vivian Maier, which I highly recommend searching out. Kaylynn Deveney's beautiful book, *The Life and Times of Albert Hastings*, inspired me to start shooting medium-format again, and it was with great excitement that I purchased *A Year of Mornings* by Maria Alexandra Vettese and Stephanie Congdon Barnes, a book that started as a blog. I'm very drawn to simplicity and natural light in photographs, and good food photography in particular is always inspiring. Check out *Super Natural Every Day* by Heidi Swanson for a book that's as delicious as the recipes it contains.

Finally, if you want to learn more about instant photography, it would be remiss of me not to mention *Instant Love: How to Make Magic and Memories with Polaroids*, the book I co-authored with Jenifer Altman and Amanda Gilligan. I hear it's not too bad.

love & gratitude

To my mum, Diane, for believing in me when I didn't.

To my sister, Abby, for being my best friend and soul mate.

To my nephew, Noah, for teaching me how to love again.

To Jim and Steve, for loving my mum and sister as much as I do.

To Madeleine, for catching me when I first fell.

To Jill, for helping me sew myself back together.

To Denise, for reaching out across an ocean.

To Denise, Letha, Liz, Megg, Michelle, and Thea, for Seattle.

To Marianne, for being my faith-keeper.

To Emma, Jo, Leonie, Lisa, Megg, Penny, and Sas, for being my Brit babes and cheerleaders.

To Nikki Hardin, for being my fairy godmother and for asking to see a book proposal.

To my editor, Mary Norris, for taking a chance on this book, and editing with such a lightness of touch.

To Kristen Mellitt, for being my book doula.

To my agent, Laura Nolan, for taking care of me so brilliantly.

To every single one of my blog readers, for your kindness and support over the years—thank you so much.

To all my amazing Unravellers, for trusting me to guide you along a new path—thank you for your bravery and honesty.

And last, but in no way least, to my love, for going first. Thank you for shining the light so I could see again.

her nephew around the garden, having lunch with friends, and plotting her next trip abroad. She likes taking photographs of her feet in various places and situations, and maintains that feet shots can often be more revealing than face shots (if you meet her don't be surprised if she points her camera at your shoes).

You can read more about her shenanigans on her blog at www.susannahconway.com.

about the author

Susannah Conway was born in 1973 in Surrey, England. She
is a photographer and writer, and has been conducting a passionate affair with instant film ever since she bought her first
Polaroid camera in 2008. A former fashion editor and freelance journalist, she is the coauthor of *Instant Love: How to Make
Magic and Memories with Polaroids* (Chronicle Books, 2012). Her
photography and writing have appeared in many international
publications including *Cosmopolitan*, *Nova*, the *Independent on
Sunday*, and the *Guardian*.

Since launching online in January 2009, the Unravelling
course has reached thousands of women all over the world. The
eight-week course uses photography assignments and writing
exercises to take participants deeper into their lives, helping
them remember who they are, where they're going, and what's
important to them—both creatively and emotionally. When
Unravellers come together, an online tribe is formed, and the
encouragement and fellowship found in the group support each
person in their own journey.

Susannah lives in Bath, England, alongside an extensive
collection of midcentury kitchenware and far too many books.
When she's not teaching or writing, she can be found chasing